GIGGING

The Musician's Underground Touring Directory

GIGGING

The Musician's Underground Touring Directory

Edited by
Michael Ethan Dorf
& Robert Appel

Writer's
Digest
Books

Cincinnati, Ohio

**Gigging: The Musician's Underground Touring
Directory.** Copyright © 1989 by Michael E. Dorf. Printed
and bound in the United States of America. All rights
reserved. No part of this book may be reproduced in any
form or by any electronic or mechanical means including
information storage and retrieval systems without
permission in writing from the publisher, except by a
reviewer, who may quote brief passages in a review.
Published by Writer's Digest Books, an imprint of F&W
Publications, Inc., 1507 Dana Ave., Cincinnati, Ohio
45207. First edition.

93 92 91 90 89   5 4 3 2 1

Library of Congress Cataloging-in-Publication Data

Gigging: the musician's underground touring directory/
edited by Michael Ethan Dorf and Robert Appel.
   p. cm.
  ISBN 0-89879-356-4
  1. Popular music—United States—Directories. 2.
Popular music—Canada—Directories. 3. Popular
music—Vocational guidance. 4. Radio stations—United
States—Directories. 5. Radio stations—Canada—
Directories. 6. Music-halls (Variety theaters, cabarets,
etc.)—United States—Directories. 7. Music-halls
(Variety theaters, cabarets, etc.)—Canada—Directories.
I. Dorf, Michael Ethan.   II. Appel, Robert.
ML17.G53 1989   89-16658
781.64'023'73—dc20   CIP
                             MN

Cover photo: Marion Appel
Design by Barbara Seitz

The editors wish to extend special thanks to the following people for their contributions to this book: Jerry A. Leibowitz, Linda Kietzer, Claudia Rowe, Laura Rothensal, Mark Williams, Steve Marsh, our editors Julie Whaley and Perri Weinberg-Schenker, and all the people who sent us pertinent information.

TABLE OF CONTENTS

Introduction

This is not, and cannot be, the definitive book on gigging in North America. It does not deal with jazz, classical, country, or straight-ahead blues. It is for artists and bands frequently labeled *alternative, progressive, new wave,* or *underground* — often because no one has heard their music before. Of course, within each of these categories is great variety. For example, hard rock and "creative pop" could certainly both be termed progressive. However, if it is "underground" music — regardless of its message, intent, or orientation — the road to success is just as arduous as it is for any mainstream band aiming for the #1 spot on any chart, if not more so.

Take Flaming Pie Records, for example.

Bob Appel and I started Flaming Pie in Wisconsin in 1984. Bob was in the band Swamp Thing, and I got involved after the band members had borrowed money from their parents to make recordings in a small studio. I made copies of the tape and went on a road trip to New York. After Swamp Thing's demo tape was rejected by all the labels in New York — majors and independents — we decided to press a record ourselves and go through the independent channels of distribution. All the members of Swamp Thing and I worked diligently at finding the names of radio stations, music presses, and clubs — anywhere we could send the album. It was the summer of 1985 when Swamp Thing and I went on our first road tour, destined to become Rock 'N' Roll Stars.

Well, our first one-month tour lost about $1,500, and if Visa hadn't extended my credit line, who knows what would have happened! We toured for about a year; the band would hit the road, play a string of shows in the Midwest, Great Lakes, the Midsouth, and usually return home with nothing more than $10 in each member's pockets. However, all this gigging around proved an extremely fruitful time for accumulating information. When the band did a show and met other bands, we always exchanged names of clubs and radio stations. I collected as much of this information as possible and followed it up with a lot of phone calls to fill out these accumulated tidbits, leads, and helpful hints.

Flaming Pie then released a compilation album of Madison, Wisconsin bands, called *The Mad Scene.* It did wonderfully in Wisconsin but sold approximately 87 albums around the world. For some ludicrous reason, this meager success inspired Bob and me to take the record company more seriously. So after borrowing money from my grandparents and Bob's father, I moved to New York City in the summer of 1986, while Bob and the band continued to be headquartered in Wisconsin. Even though Swamp Thing had a loyal following in Madison, it started concentrating more and more time, energy, and money on gigging in Philadelphia, Boston, and New York. These seemed to be the most important markets if the band was ever going to "make it" on the national front.

While I ran the label from my East Village apartment, Swamp Thing came east to record the band's second record. It went into a studio to make a very expensive piece of vinyl. At this point, Flaming Pie also signed two other Madison bands: Honor Among Thieves, and Phil Gnarly and the Tough Guys, as well as a native New Yorker, Joey Arias. During this whole period the only thing the record label seemed to collect was information, not cash.

I needed another source of income and opened a small performance space that served coffee and tea and provided a workroom for the record label in the back office. The space was a dirty old Avon Products office on Houston Street, and the first thing to be renovated was the back office where Flaming Pie was to spend more and more money trying to sell records and get gigs around the country for its bands. (It was in that office, while the rest of the space was being renovated, that we assembled, typeset, and printed the first edition of this guide on our ancient MacIntosh computer.)

The performance space was called the Knitting Factory, and the first band to play on the stage was, of course, Swamp Thing. It was also one of the last gigs Swamp Thing ever did, because Bob was getting more and more involved with the club. It took a couple of months, but by May of 1987 we were putting on music seven nights a week. Now, the *New York Times* calls us "one of new music's most important outlets."

We know (only from personal experience) that all the touring and gigging and avid self-promoting are typical and necessary for any band out there that wants to play original music (and doesn't happen to have an in with MTV). A band must do some serious road-tripping before it can expect to turn any heads. Unfortunately, the venues for alternative groups to perform in are as volatile as Frank Sinatra's temper. In some cases, a cool club may only stay open for a few months. Between the time this sentence is written and the day you read it, many of the venues listed here may go under. At the same time, a great number of new clubs will open to ever-curious crowds.

In this guide, we hope to provide information enabling ambitious musicians to pick up the ball and run with it. More than enough material is in here relating to booking, contracting, advertising, and promotion for any industrious person to further a client's musical career, or get his or her own act together. Whether you want to book a sixty-date tour across the country or just want to improve your regional contacts, this book is for you. A lot of talented musicians are out there who just need a little incentive to get out of their garages and gig in public. There are also lots of groups playing regularly who need to expand their contacts in other parts of the country. We hope this book helps all of those people, and anyone else interested in an independent musical route across the country.

How to Use This Book

The first section of this book contains articles discussing various aspects of gigging and the alternative music industry. The second section comprises the guide. It's divided geographically by areas on this continent (The Deep South, The Northeast, etc.). Each of these areas is sectioned alphabetically by state, and each state is organized alphabetically by city. Within cities are these categories: venues, record stores, radio stations, press. If a city has listings in more than one category, it gets its own subsection. At the end of each state, miscellaneous (but important) contacts are listed alphabetically. There are supportive record stores (important places to put up posters of your gigs, as well as being indispensable communications outlets for new music), radio stations, and, finally, the press. We have listed the contact person wherever possible, and sometimes the contact person's title. The indy (independent) buyer at a record store is the person who buys independently produced records. The record buyer (or LP buyer) is the general buyer for the store. Any time someone offered us a relevant tip or comment, we included that as well. Sometimes people indicate a style of music they specialize in, for your information.

The intent of this book is to enable artists to plan a tour wisely by sending their material to the appropriate people in each area they plan to hit. This is not an absolutely comprehensive list. You may even have to take the initiative and do some of your own filling-in in certain cities. But we have included enough information to help you book a tour coast-to-coast. We hope you will find the guide helpful in pursuing your artistic as well as business endeavors.

Getting the Gig: Exposure and Promotion

Perhaps you have a following in your local bar or club and your shows are progressively becoming better attended. This concentration in one place is important for development, but getting out of town and playing to strangers is also important. In fact, going on the road seems to be, with few exceptions, the only way new bands are able to get the exposure and following necessary to "make it" these days. The other possibility is to relocate to New York or the surrounding areas and get lucky. But even in New York the issues are the same.

Exposure is the key element to "making it." So many undiscovered artists are unable to share their talents only because they lack exposure. Sad but true, sometimes a band has to go to a city or a small town and run naked through the streets before anyone acknowledges its presence. It becomes very frustrating to mail your music to some local radio station that doesn't even look at it—tapes sometimes get absent-mindedly shelved. You may not have good attendance at your gigs in a town where you can't get airplay. Nevertheless, even playing for five or six people who are new listeners can pay off in the long run.

There is no real test to tell whether a band's stuff will be received favorably. Music is open to so many interpretations that saying what's "good" or what will "make it" is arbitrary. With the technological contributions to music in the last few years, the possibilities for innovation are infinite, but setting yourself apart from other bands is a very important task. Although streaking may not be the answer, it can certainly turn a lot of heads. The bottom line is that every artist should do whatever he or she can, short of overextending financial and emotional resources, to explore every possible route of exposure imaginable.

What does this involve? Basically, it means booking gigs, putting posters on everything that doesn't move, doing all the radio interviews you can, and playing on street corners to advertise on the day of your show. Also, securing a listing in the club's calendar of upcoming events and inviting press as guests to the show are two essential points for those bands hoping to be reviewed.

Radio

Airplay is ultimately the most important way a musician communicates with his or her audience. In the United States, many stations connected with colleges will play independently released records. It is enormously difficult to get any airplay on commercial radio in the United States.

5
■

CMJ (College Media Journal) helps unify the college stations in support of underground music. The college stations range from cables running between dorm rooms to stations with thousands of watts that compete with commercial AOR (album-oriented rock) stations. In some cities, listener-sponsored stations fill the void for independent music. Long Island Radio in New York and WXRT in Chicago come to mind as stations that can give an unknown band regional success.

All these stations are obviously important outlets for noncommercial bands. Most of them will not only mention the gigs in and around the city but will give some extra airplay to touring bands that are coming to town.

Postering

Postering is essential for promoting gigs because it's inexpensive and allows maximum creativity. Five hundred fluorescent yellow pieces of paper stuck to every street lamp, corner store, mailbox, bus stop, construction sight, kiosk, or street bum are very effective performance promoters. The basic technique of applying these posters involves masking tape or a staple gun. Different cities have different laws regarding where and how you can put up posters. However, there are a few places, such as New York City, where anything goes. The most common adhesive artillery in The Big Apple is wallpaper paste. First, coat the object. Next, put the poster in place. Then, slop another coat on top (the thicker the better). I've seen other methods such as using industrial glue or putting posters directly onto freshly poured sidewalk concrete. (That certainly guarantees permanence-your band's name will really stick.)

I've also been party to poster cartels where a pact is made with other poster hangers not to cover any of your posters if you'll do the same for them. Sometimes the movie poster hangers are good to get in cahoots with, because they're on the street every day and can provide a quasi-blanket of security over your posters.

The problem is one of ethics when you come to a street corner with a ton of posters stuck to the wall. The temptation is to rip down as many as possible and stick five of yours up there at eye level. That's especially tempting if yours are cool and theirs are tacky — even more tempting when theirs are out of date and your gig is coming up the next night. Since you must do something, put yours over the out-of-date ones and leave the upcoming ones in place. If all theirs are upcoming events, we suggest finding another wall. Nevertheless, certain production companies regularly hog all the best wall space by putting 10,000 tacky posters in a few blocks. In that case, no route other than retaliation seems possible. This is where your own personally drawn line of right and wrong must come into play—juvenile or not.

Exposure is open to ingenuity and prowess. Perhaps it means a local fan would call up the radio station requesting your group's record every day the week before a gig. Maybe it means opening for The Ding Dongs in the White Tuxedos if they're a big draw—even if they aren't your ideal match musically. Balancing one's artistic abilities with business ingenuity doesn't necessarily mean selling out. Each group must define where it draws the line, be it with platform shoes or bow ties.

Press Kits

So how do you convince a club owner or booking agent that your band deserves a gig? Clubs get hundreds of tapes a month—why should they book you?

Obviously, if the music you make is good, that helps. But unfortunately, there's more to it than that. A club owner must deal with the harsh reality that if no one comes to the club, no one will drink beer, and then there's no money to pay the rent. So besides the tape, the package you send to a club should include posters and flyers from your past gigs, as well as some sort of articulately written description of the band (written by a third party). Press clippings and reviews are impressive. In fact, a strong press kit can get your demo off the shelf and into the tape deck. Show your originality in how *you* work to get people to the shows. Show your mailing list. In other words, convince the club owner that you're working for him or her to get people into the club.

Sometimes the whole process seems like a Catch-22. How can you get a gig without some press or a following, but how can you get press or a following without a gig? There is no question that this is a difficult process, but you should take what you can. Opening up for a larger name act can be a great break. Even for no money, the benefits of playing for a crowd that you otherwise wouldn't have are invaluable. There is your chance for a possible review. There is no telling what good can come out of exposing your music to unknown, potentially supportive audiences.

Getting Paid for the Gig

While radio play, record deals, and screaming fans are nice, getting paid for a gig at the end of the night puts rice and beans on the table. Too many groups have been ripped off by either greedy promoters or their own financial carelessness. Contracts, and an understanding of the structure of normal deals, will help alleviate some of the associated problems.

The two ends of the financial spectrum are the *flat fee* or the *percentage of the door*. You might be offered $100 flat to do a show. In that case, even if the club ends up collecting $10,000 at the door, you will be paid $100. The other extreme is a straight percentage, but 90 percent of $20 collected is only $18. So generally a combination of the two, in the form of a guarantee vs. a percentage of the door, is the accepted norm. The guarantee should at least cover the band's expenses so that even if the show is a bomb, there's some money to pay for the gas.

The percentage of the door will fluctuate according to a number of variables. The more the club wants the *band* to do the promotion and work in drawing a crowd, the larger the percentage relative to the guarantee will be. The more the club thinks it can capitalize with the band's draw, the smaller the percentage relative to the guarantee will be.

The percentage can be expressed in the language of *vs.* or *plus* the guarantee. Say the guarantee is $250 *vs.* 100 percent of the door. If the cover is $5 and 100 people pay at the door, the band gets $500 because that's larger than the guarantee. If 40 people show up, the $200 taken in at the door is less than the guarantee; therefore, take the $250 and go home.

Sometimes the deal is expressed in terms of *plus* the guarantee. In other words, the compensation will be the base guarantee *plus* a percentage of the door, regardless of the expenses. This might be offered if the club owner feels a need to give the band some percentage but allows room for the club to make a bundle if there's a big turnout. Each agreement varies with the circumstances. Clearly, if a band can promote the hell out of a show and feels confident about a big draw, it should ask for a majority percentage of the door. If its playing in a city for the first time and can't really do much advance promotion, it should try for a larger guarantee.

Of course, there's the situation of a club drawing a large crowd every night because there's some sort of "scene" happening there. In this case, the owner knows that the band is incidental to the pulling power of the club itself, in which case there's no reason to give away any percentage of the door. In this scenario, a flat fee is usually paid to the band. It might have been more profitable playing for a percentage of the door, but the benefits of playing to a larger crowd in a well-known club are immeasurable.

There's a growing trend for clubs to ask bands to guarantee a certain turnout at their performances. This is an economical consideration — they want to give new bands a chance, but they don't want to allow unknown bands to play and actually lose money when they could have booked a well-known band and made a killing. If you're offered this kind of a deal, you'll have to really promote your show and be able to draw the crowd yourself. So don't be unrealistic and brag about the millions of people dying to come hear you play. Decide whether it's worth it to possibly lose money if you have to pay the club owner what he or she didn't take in at the door. How confident are you that you can do the promotion to draw the crowd? How badly do you need this gig? Are you willing to buy exposure? It could be that if you play for clubs under these circumstances a couple of times, you'll draw a bigger and bigger crowd and ultimately be able to negotiate for a higher fee.

In the end, each financial decision becomes a unique one depending on a variety of factors. It's the subjective analysis or, in some cases, the shot-in-the-dark logic of the person doing the booking, that determines whether a band gets a fair deal.

Contracts

Contracts offer a method to help ensure things happen the way they were expected to by both the band and the club owner. Because most of the people involved in this business have done, or continue to do, the kinds of activities that hamper the fastidious functionings of the memory, putting down the essentials of a gig on paper is a good thing to do.

Even between friends, certain items in a deal can be forgotten or overlooked — a written contract can be, at the very minimum, a reminder to bring two cases of beer and not one to the gig. But more importantly, contracts can be used to enforce the terms of an arrangement instead of having shows thousands of miles from home depend upon one phone conversation.

The band Killdozer, from Madison, Wisconsin, had a problem that illustrates this point very clearly. The members made arrangements a number of years ago for their first tour out west with some guy in San Francisco. This guy, let's call him A. Painindabut, says he can put a complete package together for them with a few dates in Los Angeles, San Francisco, and some other California cities. So they negotiate with Mr. Painindabut a "guarantee" of $500 per show to cover their expenses out to California from Madison. So everything was set, and off they went in their rented van. They arrived in San Francisco three days later and called Mr. Painindabut, whose roommate informed them that he just left town. They called the club, and there was another band scheduled. The club claimed it never even heard of the band Killdozer. So here they were in California, 2,000 miles from home, with no money, no place to stay, and they'd sunk their last dough into the van, gas, and food. Well, they had no choice but to use their Visa cards and drive all the way back to Wisconsin.

Killdozer isn't the only band this has happened to. In fact, most bands have similar horror stories about A. Painindabut to relate to one another backstage. A lot of these rip-offs can be avoided by a simple contract. Although a contract doesn't get your pay from the Mafia, it will guarantee the fulfillment of obligations in most situations.

The following page contains a simple contract highlighting most of the provisions that are important at this stage of the game. At some point, more lengthy riders will need to be attached describing in sordid detail the type of gazpacho soup or vintage St. Emillion that is absolutely necessary to consume before properly performing in front of an audience. But until that point, the following can be enlarged and copied for your use:

Musician's Contract Rider

This contract is for the personal services of_____ (herein called "artist") and_____ (herein called "purchaser") for the engagement described below is made this_____, 19__, between the undersigned artist and purchaser.

1. Place of Venue_____

2. Date(s) of Show_____

3. Times: Load in_____ Sound Check_____ Start_____

4. Number and Length of sets_____

5. Sound System:_____

_____

6. Compensation Agreed upon: Services_____

                             Lodging_____

                             Meals_____

                             Transportation_____

                             Other_____

      Total_____

7. Payment to be made either □ in cash or □ by check no later than_____

8. Sales of Paraphernalia by artists will be on the following terms:_____

_____

9. Other_____

_____

10. The recording, reproduction, or transmission of Artist's performance is prohibited absent written consent of Artist. 11. Artist's obligations under this contract are subject to detention or prevention by sickness, accident, riots, strikes, epidemics, or any other Act of God which could endanger the health or safety of the Artist. 12. If any of the artist's compensation is to be based on the door receipts, a) the purchaser agrees to provide the artist a statement of the gross receipts within two hours of the conclusion of the performance if asked and b) Artist shall have the right to have representation at the door or the box office at all times, and said representation shall have the right to examine box office records relating to the performance only. 13. In the event purchaser fails to fulfill its obligation provided herein, purchaser will be liable to Artist in addition to the compensation provided herein. 14. Either party may cancel this agreement without obligation to other if notice is received 21 days in advance of show. In witness whereof, the parties sign this contract this __ day of_____, 19____.

_____ Purchaser   _____ Artist

Accommodations on the Road

The tight budget of most bands makes staying in a hotel out of the question. The most common places to sleep, besides the floor of the sweat-smelling van, are friends' houses, the club owner's living room, etc. If you don't have any friends or acquaintances in town, then ask the people at the club if they have any floor space. Usually with the right smile and a shower within the last three days, an impassioned, poverty-stricken look will get you a reservation on a comfortable couch somewhere.

Then again, there's always the possibility that there will be no place to stay. As a last resort, Jonathan Zarov of Swamp Thing used an ingenious tactic on the first night of a tour in Philadelphia. The band had tentative reservations at a friend's house that went sour, and all the other Philly connections seemed to be of no avail. So, during the final set, among the large crowd of eleven people, Jon went up to candle-lit tables and started "getting to know" the audience — Las Vegas style. With soft cocktail music being played by the band, he related the necessity of accommodations for the evening.

As it turned out, two people offered a floor to crash on, and they ended up being devoted fans. So what looked like another night in the van turned into a great relationship and a strong liaison in a city. To show its gratitude, the band made it a habit to give away tee-shirts and records to the people it stayed with.

How Record Labels Work

You've recorded your first demo and it's just incredible. It's fantastic, it's, it's the next best thing to Phil Gnarly and the Tough Guys, or whatever. You've made a bunch of copies (twenty or fifty, or something in there), put on a suit and borrowed a tie, and peddled them around to every major label this side of Tokyo. Most of those companies with gold records gilding the walls won't even let you past the receptionist. She'll probably tell you to drop it off for Mr. Big, and he'll "get right back to you." Don't get mad at her—she's got the depressing daily job of rejecting people she doesn't even know. Even if you've got a contact or a meeting set up at a company, you'll probably end up dropping off a tape.

For most alternative or underground bands, the mailbox is as close as you'll get to a major label. The tapes get dropped into a pile of about a hundred other tapes. Sometimes they do actually get listened to by A&R people (Artists and Repertoire—the title given to talent scouts). Replies can be received in the mail up to six months after you submitted your demo. They usually sound like this: "We think this is good material, but it's not for our label at this time." Some labels won't accept unsolicited tapes at all. This is not to say that being discovered by major labels is impossible, but it's more of a hoax than reality.

The way the industry seems to be heading is similar to the minor league/major league pattern in baseball—the majors monitoring the minors for new talent. In other words, the major labels wait for a band to make a couple of records, and then they gauge the response of college radio and the press to assess the group's salability. Basically, they're letting the groups be test marketed by a smaller company before investing in the band themselves. This eliminates the risk for the big guys. Income statements become the guidelines for artistic decisions. And, for any of you out there who are really well-versed in stock market lingo; progressive/alternative bands are looked upon as incidental investments. Top 40/pop music is the blue chip stock, while nonconforming styles are seen as options.

If you look at some of the independent charts from a few years ago, you'll notice bands such as Husker D or The Replacements on the top of the list. They both had material out on independent labels before being signed to a major label deal. You have to admit it makes sense; the majors want to engage in risk-free, profitable projects as much as they can. This shouldn't be discouraging, but stimulating. It gives independents the room to be creative and to experiment with more risky forms of music. Music hasn't become stagnant at all. It's just that independent labels are taking up the slack and filling the void where the majors are afraid to venture. Certain independent labels such as SST, Sire, and I.R.S. have become increasingly important to the big guys over the years.

Contacting the A&R people at these record companies and getting them to listen to your demo are the first steps in being signed to a label deal. Keep in mind, however, that the companies listed don't necessarily accept unsolicited tapes.

Record Companies

Major Labels:

A & M Records
595 Madison Ave.
New York, NY 10022
Contact: Nancy Jeffries

A & M Records
1416 North LaBrea Ave.
Hollywood, CA 90028

Arista Records
6 West 57th Street
New York, NY 10019
Contact: Michelle Block,
Promotion

Arista Records
8370 Wilshire Blvd.
Beverly Hills, CA 90211

Atlantic Records
75 Rockefeller Plaza
New York, NY 10019
Contact: Tim Carr,
Vivian Piazz

Atlantic Records
9229 Sunset Blvd.,
Suite 710
Los Angeles, CA 90069

Capitol Records
1370 Avenue of the
Americas
New York, NY 10019

Capitol Records
1750 North Vine Street
Hollywood, CA 90028

CBS Records
1801 Century Park West
Los Angeles, CA 90069

CBS Records
51 West 52nd Street
New York, NY 10019

CBS Records
34 Music Square East
Nashville, TN 37203

Chrysalis Records
645 Madison Ave.
New York, NY 10012
Contact: Francis
Pennington

Chrysalis Records
9255 Sunset Blvd.
Los Angeles, CA 90069

**Elektra/Asylum/
Nonesuch Records**
75 Rockefeller Plaza
New York, NY 10019
Contact: Sherry Ring,
Publicity

**Elektra/Asylum/
Nonesuch Records**
9229 Sunset Blvd.
Los Angeles, CA 90069

Epic Records
(see CBS Records)

Gaia
(see Gramavision
Records)

Geffen Records
9126 Sunset Blvd.
Los Angeles, CA 90069
Contact: Mark Kates

Geffen Records
75 Rockefeller Plaza
New York, NY 10019

Gramavision Records
121 West 27th Street
New York, NY 1001

IRS Records
100 Universal City Place
University City, CA
91608
Contact: Lori
Blumenthal or Annie
Fort

IRS Records
1755 Broadway,
Eighth Floor
New York, NY 10019

Island Records
14 East Fourth St., Third
Floor
New York, NY 10012
Contact: Chris Reade or
Chris Merola

Island Records
6525 Sunset Blvd.,
Second Floor
Los Angeles, CA 90028

Manhattan Records
1370 Avenue of the
Americas
New York, NY 10019
Contact: Bruce Garfield

MCA Records
70 Universal City Place
University City, CA
91608

MCA Records
445 Park Ave.
New York, NY 10022

Mercury
(see PolyGram Records,
Inc.)

Motown Records
(see MCA Records)

Polydor
(see PolyGram Records,
Inc.)

**PolyGram Records,
Inc.**
810 Seventh Ave.
New York, NY 10019

**PolyGram Records,
Inc.**
8335 Sunset Blvd.
Los Angeles, CA 90028

RCA Records
1133 Avenue of the
Americas
New York, NY 10036
Contact: John Siglerb or
Marilyn Lipsius

RCA Records
6363 Sunset Blvd.
Hollywood, CA 90028

Reprise
(see Warner Bros.
Records)

Sire Records
(see Warner Bros.
Records)

Slash Records
7381 Beverly Blvd.
Los Angeles, CA 90036
Contact: Jason Luckitt
or Michelle Craig

Virgin
9247 Alden Drive
Beverly Hills, CA 90210

Virgin
30 West 21st Street
New York, NY 10010
Contact: Todd Bisson or
Paul Brown

Warner Bros. Records
75 Rockefeller Plaza
New York, NY 10019
Contact: Mary Milea

Warner Bros. Records
3300 Warner Blvd.
Burbank, CA 91505

Warner Bros. Records
1815 Division Street
P.O. Box 120897
Nashville, TN 37212

Big Independent Labels

Alligator Records
P.O. Box 60234
Chicago, IL 60660

Alternative Tentacles
P.O. Box 11458
San Francisco, CA 94101

**Barking Pumpkin
Records**
P.O. Box 5265
North Hollywood, CA
91616

Celluloid Records
330 Hudson, Fourth
Floor
New York, NY 10013
Contact: Gordy Gillespie

Curb Records
3907 West Alameda
Avenue, Second Floor
Burbank, CA 91505

EG Records
P.O. Box 51298
New York, NY 10185
Contact: Ellen Frank

EMI-Manhattan
6920 Sunset Blvd.
Los Angeles, CA 90028
Contact: Milham Gorky,
Publicity

EMI-Manhattan
1370 Avenue of the
Americas
New York, NY 10019

Enigma Records
1750 East Holly Ave.
El Segundo, CA 90245
Contact: Juli Kryslur or
Lynn Oaks

Fundamental Music
P.O. Box 2309
San Francisco, CA 94107
Contact: Richard Jordan

Homestead Records
P.O. Box 570
Rockville Centre, NY
11571
Contact: Gerald Cosloy

Madam Records
P.O. Box 988
San Francisco, CA 94101

Profile Records
740 Broadway, Seventh
Floor
New York, NY 10003
Contact: Chris LaSalle
or Tracy Miller

PVC/JEM
3619 Kennedy Road
South Plainfield, NJ
07080

Relativity Records
187-07 Henderson Ave.
Hollis, NY 11423

Relativity Records
1830 West 208th Street
Torrance, CA 90501

Rhino Records
2225 Colorado Ave.
Santa Monica, CA 90404
Contact: Tracy Mann
Hill

Rough Trade
326 Sixth Street
San Francisco, CA 94103

Rounder Records
1 Camp Street
Cambridge, MA 02140

**Shanachie Records
Corp.**
Dalebrook Park Dept.
Hohokus, NY 07423
Contact: Randall Gross

SST Records
P.O. Box 1
Lawndale, CA 90260
Contact: Michael
Whitaker

Tommy Boy Records
1747 First Ave.
New York, NY 10128
Contact: Joseph Gardner

Twin/Tone Records
2541 Nicollet Ave. South
Minneapolis, MN 55404

Small Independent Labels

Ameba Records
5337 LaCresta Court
Los Angeles, CA 90038-4001

Azra Records
P.O. Box 459
Maywood, CA 90270
Contact: David Richards

Baby Sue Records
P.O. Box 1111
Decatur, GA 30031

Big Chief Records
54 West 16th Street
New York, NY 10011

Blue Island Records
P.O. Box 171265
San Diego, CA 92117-0975

Bomp Records
P.O. Box 7112
Burbank, CA 91510

Buddah Records Inc.
1790 Broadway
New York, NY 10019
Contact: Phil Kahl

Carlyle Records
1217 16th Ave. South
Nashville, TN 37212
Contact: Preston Brogdon

Caroline Records Inc.
5 Crosby Street
New York, NY 10013
Contact: Robert Conroy

Cryptovision
P.O. Box 1812
New York, NY 10009

Cuneiform Records
P.O. Box 6517
Wheaton, MD 20906-0517

Dischord Records
3819 Beecher Street
Northwest
Washington, D.C. 10007

Distraught Records
11602 Poplarwood
Houston, TX 77089
Contact: Rodney

Dr. Dream Records
58 Plaza Square, Suite G
Orange, CA 92666

Eubet Records
6923 Clarendon Road D-4
Bethesda, MD 20814

Fast Track Records
264 Tosca Drive
Stoughton, MA 02072
Contact: Michael Glassman

Forecast Records
1765 Highland Ave.
Los Angeles, CA 90028

415 Records
P.O. Box 14563
San Francisco, CA 94114
Contact: Howie Klein

Gelatinous Records
P.O. Box 10023
Arlington, VA 22210

GGE Records
P.O. Box 5088
Kent, OH 44240

Green Money Records
P.O. Box 31983
Seattle, WA 98103

Headstrong Records
P.O. Box 3173
Princeton, NJ 08543

Hopewell Records
P.O. Box 3131
Princeton, NJ 08540

Iloki Records
P.O. Box 49593
Los Angeles, CA 90049

Independent Label Alliance
P.O. Box 594M
Bayshore, NY 11706
Contact: Jim Reynolds

Invasion Group Records
114 Lexington Ave., Third Floor
New York, NY 10016
Contact: Peter Casperson or John Scott

Jet Records
8730 Sunset Blvd., #200
Los Angeles, CA 90069
Contact: Pat Siciliano

Kapital Records
P.O. Box 1031
Adelaide Street Station
Toronto, Ontario M5C 2K4

Link Records
277 Church Street, Third Floor
New York, NY 10013
Contact: John Hudson

Live Wire Records
P.O. Box 1222
Santa Fe, NM 87504

Lovely Music Ltd.
325 Spring Street
New York, NY 10013
Contact: John Ashley

Mad Rover Records
P.O. Box 22243
Sacramento, CA 95822
Contact: John Bacciagaluppi

MB3
330 West 46th Street
New York, NY 10036

MCF Records
3361½ Cahuenga Blvd.
West Hollywood, CA 90068

Melted Records
618 Willow Ave.
Hoboken, NJ 07030

Mercenary Records
330 Hudson, Fourth Floor
New York, NY 10013

Midnight Records
P.O. Box 390
Old Chelsea Station
New York, NY 10011

Mirror Records Inc.
645 Titus Ave.
Rochester, NY 14617
Contact: Armand Schaubroeck

Motiv
Communications
P.O. Box 875422
Los Angeles, CA 90087

Panagaea Records
1776 Broadway
New York, NY 10019

Perimeter Records
P.O. Box 28882
Atlanta, GA 30358-0882

Placebo Records
P.O. Box 23316
Phoenix, AZ 85063

Poindexter Records
1916 Perry Street
Durham, NC 27705

Pop Records
P.O. Box 108
Tampa, FL 33601
Contact: Steve Tinsky

Post Mortem Records
P.O. Box 358
New Milford, NJ 07646

Pravda Records
3728 North Clark Street
Chicago, IL 60613

Private Music
220 East 23rd Street
New York, NY 10012
Contact: Ron Goldstein
or Beth Louis

Raven
1005 Carpenter Street
Philadelphia, PA 19147

Riti Records
P.O. Box 1252
Cambridge, MA 02238

Rock Bottom Records
P.O. Box 1315
Boston, MA 02104

Silent Records
540 Alabama, #310
San Francisco, CA 94110

South East Records
208 Davenport
Iowa City, IA 52240

Speechless Records
P.O. Box 373
Pasadena, MD 21122

Subelecktric Inst.
475 21st Ave.
San Francisco, CA 94121

Suite Beat Music
3355 West El Segundo
Hawthorne, CA 90250

Sutra Records/Buddah
Records
1 Madison Ave.
New York, NY 10010

Taang Records
P.O. Box 51
Auburndale, MA 02166
Contact: Curtis

Touch and Go Records
P.O. Box 433
Dearborn, MI 48121

TVT Records
59 West 19th Street,
Suite 5B
New York, NY 10011
Contact: Steve Gottleib
or Kitty Overton

Victory Records
P.O. Box 38943
Houston, TX 77238-8943

Wind & Sound Records
50 West 34th Street,
#11C5
New York, NY 10001

World Artists
P.O. Box 63
Orinda, CA 94563
Contact: J. Malcolm
Baird

Yet You Records
4252 Melrose
Hollywood, CA 90029

CALIFORNIA

C A L I F O R N I A

Berkeley

Venues

Berkeley Square
1333 University Ave.
Berkeley, CA 94702
415-849-3374
Contact: Michael

Record Stores

Rasputins Records
2333 Telegraph Ave.
Berkeley, CA 94704
415-848-9004
Contact: Steve Berchtold

Tower Records
2510 Durant Ave.
Berkeley, CA 94704
Indy Buyer
415-841-0101
Takes records on consignment if band is getting airplay.

Radio Stations

KALX
University of California
2311 Bowditch
Berkeley, CA 94704
415-642-1111

KPFA
2207 Shattuck Ave.
Berkeley, CA 94704
415-848-6767

Press

Daily Californian
2150 Dwight Way
Berkeley, CA 94704
415-548-8405
Contact: J. Poet, Music Editor

Chico

Record Stores

Sundance Records
218 Broadway
Chico, CA 95928
Contact: Rick
916-893-4303

Tower Records
215 Main Street
Chico, CA 95928
916-345-8582
Contact: Lynn Brown

Radio Stations

KCSC
California State University
P.O. Box 1580
Chico, CA 95929
916-895-6228
Contact: Russell Damien, Program Director

Concord

Record Stores

Tower Records
1280 East Willow Pass Road
Concord, CA 94520
415-827-2900
Contact: Stephen Senishen

Radio Stations

KEGR
P.O. Box 103
2425 Hemlock Ave.
Concord, CA 94522
415-680-5347
Contact: Steve O'Brien, Program
Director

Fresno

Record Stores

Tower Records
5301 North Blackstone Ave.
Fresno, CA 93710
209-431-4700
Contact: Mike Joy

Radio Stations

KFSR
California State University-Fresno
Shaw and Maple Ave.
Fresno, CA 93740
209-294-2598
Contact: Cyndie Wathen

Hollywood

Venues

Cavern, The
6419 Hollywood Blvd.
Hollywood, CA 90028
213-227-4141
Contact: Greg Shaw
Sixties music

Club Lingerie
6507 Sunset Blvd.
Hollywood, CA 90028
213-466-8557
Contact: Brenden Myllen
Variety music
Send promo package

Gazzarri's
9039 Sunset Blvd.
Hollywood, CA 90069
213-273-6606
Contact: Michael
*Promoters rent the club, and bands
should call them: Bryan Markovitz
Productions 818-336-1615; After Dark
Productions 818-996-8131; Creative
Images Association 213-856-0823*

Palace, The
1735 Vine Street
Hollywood, CA 90028
213-462-3000, 213-462-7362
Contact: John Harrington

Palomino, The
6907 Lankershim Blvd.
Hollywood, CA 91605
818-764-4018
Contact: Billy Thomas
Variety music
Talent night every Monday night

Rajis
6160 Hollywood Blvd.
Hollywood, CA 90028
213-469-4552, 213-428-9947
Contact: Jan

Roxy, The
9009 Sunset Blvd.
Hollywood, CA 90069
213-278-9457, 213-278-2447
Call to get list of promoters
Variety music

21

Whiskey A Go Go
8901 Sunset Blvd.
Hollywood, CA 90069
213-652-4205

Record Stores

Bleecker Bob's
7663 Melrose Ave.
Hollywood, CA 90046
213-852-9444
Indy Buyer

Bug Music
6777 Hollywood Blvd., Ninth Floor
Hollywood, CA 90028
213-466-4352
Contact: Lanette Phillips

Tower Records
8801 West Sunset Blvd.
Hollywood, CA 90069
213-657-7300
Indy Buyer

Radio Stations

KNX FM
6121 Sunset Blvd.
Hollywood, CA 90028
213-460-3333

KPFK
3729 Cahuenga Blvd. West
N. Hollywood, CA 91604
818-985-2711

Irvine
Venues

Associated Students of U.C. Irvine
University Center, Room 205
University of California-Irvine
Irvine, CA 92715
714-856-0461
Contact: Lance MacLean

Radio Stations

KUCI
University of California-Irvine
P.O. Box 4362
Irvine, CA 92716-4362
714-856-6868
Contact: Gary Downs, Music
Director

Long Beach
Venues

Bogart's
6288 East Pacific Coast Hgwy.
Long Beach, CA 90803
213-594-8975
Contact: David Swinson
All music but jazz

Fender's Ballroom
530 East Broadway
Long Beach, CA 90802
213-435-6311
Contact: John Fender

Record Stores

Culture Beat
814 East Fourth Street
Long Beach, CA 90802
213-495-1181
Contact: Courtney Minors

Zed Records
1940 Lakewood Blvd.
Long Beach, CA 90815
213-498-2757
Contact: Mike Zampelli

Radio Stations

KNAC
Flagship Broadcasting
100 Ocean Gate Blvd., Suite P70
Long Beach, CA 90802
213-437-0366

Los Angeles

"80,000 bands and only a couple of places to play."
— Harlan Steinberger, local musician.

Venues

Anti Club
4658 Melrose Ave.
Los Angeles, CA 90029
213-667-9762
*Send Rock 'n' Roll tapes to: Red River,
P.O. Box 26774, Los Angeles, CA 90026*

Music Machine
12220 West Pico Blvd.
Los Angeles, CA 90064
213-820-5150

Stock Exchange
618 South Spring Street
Los Angeles, CA 90014
213-627-4400
Contact: Todd Breslau
Variety music

Record Stores

Aron's Records
7725 Melrose Ave.
Los Angeles, CA 90046
213-653-8170
Contact: Paul Rock

Barton's Records
4018 Buckingham Road
Los Angeles, CA 90008
213-298-9338
Contact: Balfour Barton

Music Plus
101 North Fairfax
Los Angeles, CA 90036
213-938-3048, 213-234-3336
Indy Buyer

Record Rover
12204 Venice Blvd.
Los Angeles, CA 90066
213390-3132
Contact: Guy Mouledoux

Record Trader
7701 Melrose Ave.
Los Angeles, CA 90046
213-653-6026
Contact: Joel Armstrong

Reggae International
4343 Crenshaw Blvd., #104
Los Angeles, CA 90008
213-292-2106
Contact: James Moorer

Rhino Records
1720 Westwood Blvd.
Los Angeles, CA 90024
213-474-3786
Contact: Jon Liu

Rockaway Records
2506 North Glendale Blvd.
Los Angeles, CA 90039
213-664-3232
Indy Buyer

Tower Records
1028 Westwood Blvd.
Los Angeles, CA 90024
213-208-3061
Indy Buyer

Vinyl Fetish
7305 Melrose Ave.
Los Angeles, CA 90046
213-935-1300
Contact: Michael Stewart

Radio Stations

KLA
University of California-Los Angeles
308 Westwood Plaza
2400 Ackerman Union
Los Angeles, CA 90024
213-825-9104

KLOS
3321 South La Cienega
P.O. Box 95.5
Los Angeles, CA 90016
213-840-4800

KSCR
University of Southern California
404 Student Union Building
Los Angeles, CA 90089-0895

KXLU
Loyola Marymount University
7101 West 80th Street
Los Angeles, CA 90045
213-642-2866

Press

Blitz
P.O. Box 48124
Los Angeles, CA 90048
818-705-4163
Contact: Mike McDowell

L.A. Reader
12224 Victory Blvd.
Los Angeles, CA 91606
213-655-8810
Contact: Natalie Nichols

L.A. Weekly
P.O. Box 29905
Los Angeles, CA 90029
213-667-2620
Contact: Jonathan Gold

Los Angeles Herald Examiner
P.O. Box 2416 Terminal Annex
1111 South Broadway
Los Angeles, CA 90015
213-744-8000
Contact: Greg Sandow, Music Editor

Los Angeles Times
Times Mirror Square
Los Angeles, CA 90053
213-237-5000
Contact: Bob Hilburn, Pop/Rock Editor

Music Connection
6640 Sunset Blvd., First Floor
Los Angeles, CA 90028
213-462-5772
Contact: Kenny Kerner, Senior Editor

Option
2345 Westwood Blvd., Suite 2
Los Angeles, CA 90064
213-474-2600
Contact: Scott Becker

Northridge

Record Stores

Tower Records
19320 Nordhoff Street
Northridge, CA 91324
818-993-4911
Indy Buyer

Radio Stations

KCSN
California State University-Northridge
18111 Nordhoff Street
Northridge, CA 91330
818-885-3090

Oakland

Venues

Hill, The
4100 Redwood Road
Oakland, CA 94619
415-530-7260
Contact: Doug Byrone
Rock 'n' Roll and Top 40

Record Stores

Astas Records
5488 College Ave.
Oakland, CA 94618
415-654-0335
Contact: Michael Conan

Press

Oakland Tribune
409 13th Street
Oakland, CA 94612
415-945-1350
Contact: Perry Phillips

Sacramento

Record Stores

Tower Records
2500 16th Street
Sacramento, CA 95818
916-444-3000
Contact: Tom Pompeii

Tower Records
5950 Florin Road
Sacramento, CA 95823
916-391-3800
Contact: Ray Kopeland

Tower Records
726 K Street
Sacramento, CA 95814
916-446-3111
Contact: Ernie Sayson

Tower Records
2514 Watt Ave.
Sacramento, CA 95821
916-482-9191
Contact: Randy Mondonza

Radio Stations

KRXQ
5301 Madison Ave., Suite 402
Sacramento, CA 95841
916-334-7777

KXPR
3416 American River Drive, Suite B
Sacramento, CA 95864
916-485-5977

San Diego

Venues

Spirit, The
1130 Buenos Ave.
San Diego, CA 92110
619-276-3993
Contact: Jerry
All kinds of music

Record Stores

Off the Record
6136 El Cajon Blvd.
San Diego, CA 92115
619-265-0507
Contact: Keith Larson

Tower Records
6405 El Cajon Blvd.
San Diego, CA 92115
619-287-1420
Contact: Bob Orozco

Tower Records
3601 Sports Arena Blvd.
San Diego, CA 92110
619-224-3333
Contact: Terry Tveraas

Radio Stations

KCR
San Diego State University
5300 Campanile Drive
San Diego, CA 92182
619-594-6280

XTRA
4891 Pacific Hgwy.
San Diego, CA 92110
619-291-9191

San Francisco

There is support for all styles of music here, not just the Grateful Dead.

Venues

Club Nine
399 Ninth Street
San Francisco, CA 94103
415-386-9745

Das Klub
1015 Folsom Street
San Francisco, CA 94103
415-626-2899
Contact: Brian

DNA Lounge
375 11th Street
San Francisco, CA 94103
415-626-1409

DV8
55 Natoma
San Francisco, CA 94105
415-777-1419
Contact: Dr. Winkie
Variety music

Hamburger Mary's
1582 Folsom Street
San Francisco, CA 94103
415-626-1985
Contact: Dale Rideout
Variety music

I-Beam
1748 Haight Street
San Francisco, CA 94117
415-668-6006, 415-665-8266
Contact: Cathy Cohn
Variety music, big on alternative bands

Kennel Club, The
628 Divisadero Street
San Francisco, CA 94117
415-931-1914
R & B, and Variety

Last Day Saloon
406 Clement Street
San Francisco, CA 94118
415-387-6343
Contact: Dave Daher
R & B, Motown, and Rock 'n' Roll

Nightbreak
1821 Haight Street
San Francisco, CA 94117
415-221-9008
Contact: Jimmy Lyons

Oasis, The
1369 Folsom Street
San Francisco, CA 94103
415-621-8119
Contact: Gary Walker
Variety music

Stone, The
412 Broadway
San Francisco, CA 94133
415-391-8284
Contact: Bobby Corona or Melvin
Brown
All kinds of music

Record Stores

Aquarius Music
3961 24th Street
San Francisco, CA 94114
415-647-2272
Contact: Patrick

101 Music
1414 Grant Ave.
San Francisco, CA 94133
415-392-6369
Indy Buyer

Rainbow Records
379 Oyster Point Blvd., Building 5
San Francisco, CA 94080
415-952-3560
Contact: Tom McCaffrey

Reckless Records
1401 Haight Street
San Francisco, CA 94117
415-431-3434
Contact: Jeff Parker

Record Finder
258 Noe Street
San Francisco, CA 94114
415-431-4443
Contact: Richard Rohde

Revolver Records
520 Clement Street
San Francisco, CA 94118
415-386-6128
Contact: Jeff Davis

Rough Trade Record Store
326 Sixth Street
San Francisco, CA 94103
415-621-4045/4307, 415-863-8829
Contact: Uli

Streetlight Records
3979 24th Street
San Francisco, CA 94114
415-282-3550
Contact: Mark Weinstein

Streetlight Records
2350 Market Street
San Francisco, CA 94114
415-282-8000
Contact: Tom

Tower Records
2525 Jones, Columbus, and Bay
San Francisco, CA 94133
415-885-0500
Contact: Wayne

Used Record Shoppe
1325 Ninth Ave.
San Francisco, CA 94122
415-665-2055
Contact: Bob Stuber
Takes records on consignment

Radio Stations

KCSF
P.O. Box A160
50 Phelan Ave.
San Francisco, CA 94117
415-239-3444

KFOG
55 Green Street
San Francisco, CA 94111
415-986-1045

KKHI
St. Francis Hotel
335 Powell Street
San Francisco, CA 94102
415-986-2151

KQED
500 Eighth Street
San Francisco, CA 94103
415-553-2129

KSFS
San Francisco State University
1600 Holloway Ave.
San Francisco, CA 94132
415-469-2428, 415-338-2428

KUSF
2130 Fulton Street
San Francisco, CA 94117
415-386-5873

WARD
Western Association of Rock Disc
Jockeys
405 Shrader Street
San Francisco, CA 94117
415-668-0900

Press

San Francisco Chronicle
901 Mission Street
San Francisco, CA 94103
Contact: Bob Graham, A & E Editor,
Joel Selvin, Music Critic

Thrasher
P.O. Box 884570
San Francisco, CA 94188-4570
415-822-3083
Contact: Brian Schroeder
Monthly publication

Vinyl Propaganda
405 Shrader Street
San Francisco, CA 94117
415-668-0900
Contact: Sam LaBelle, Editor
Monthly magazine

San Jose

Venues

Cabaret, The
370 South Sarratoga Ave.
San Jose, CA 95129
408-248-0643
Contact: Marlin Nicks
Variety music

Oasis
200 N. First Street
San Jose, CA 95113
408-292-2212
Contact: Steve Hoey
Modern, punk, and rock

Radio Stations

KOME
3031 Tisch Way, Suite #3
San Jose, CA 95128
408-985-9800

KSJO
1420 Koll Circle
San Jose, CA 95112
408-288-5400

KSJS
San Jose State University
San Jose, CA 95192-0094
408-924-4548

Record Stores

Streetlight Records
535 South Bascom Ave.
San Jose, CA 95128
408-292-1404
Contact: Jeff Riedle

San Juan Capistrano

Venues

Coach House, The
33157 Camino Capistrano
San Juan Capistrano, CA 92675
714-496-8930
Contact: Ken Phebus or Nikki Sweet

Record Stores

Condor Records
32341 Camino Capistrano
San Juan Capistrano, CA 92675
714-496-2425
Contact: Ron Martin

San Luis Obispo

Venues

Dark Room, The
1037 Monterey Street
San Luis Obispo, CA 93401
805-543-5131
Contact: Jack Kinney
Variety music

Record Stores

Big Music
1817 B. Osos Street
San Louis Obispo, CA 93401
805-543-8164
Contact: Bob O'Brien

Boo Boo Records
978 Monterey Street
San Luis Obispo, CA 93401
805-541-0657
Contact: Mike White

Cheap Thrills Records
873 Marsh
San Luis Obispo, CA 93401
805-544-0686
Contact: Elwood Thompson

Radio Stations

KCPR
Graphic Arts 201
California Polytechnical Institute
San Luis Obispo, CA 93407
805-544-4640, 805-756-2965

KPGA
3195 McMillan Road, Suite G
San Luis Obispo, CA 93401
805-773-1895

Press

New Times
738 Higuera
P.O. Box 13638
San Luis Obispo, CA 93401
805-546-8208
Contact: Steve Moss, Editor
Weekly newspaper

Telegram Tribune
P.O. Box 112
1321 Johnson Ave.
San Luis Obispo, CA 93406
805-595-1111
Contact: Tony Hazarian
Saturday calendar lists gigs

San Mateo

Record Stores

Tower Records
2727 South El Camino Real
San Mateo, CA 94403
415-570-4600
Contact: Paul Bunch

Radio Stations

KSCM
1700 West Hillsdale Blvd.
San Mateo, CA 94402
415-574-6427

Santa Clara

Venues

One Step Beyond
1400 Martin Ave.
Santa Clara, CA 95050
408-727-0901
Contact: Stan Kent
Alternative modern rock 'n' roll

Radio Stations

KSCU
P.O. Box 1207
Santa Clara University
Santa Clara, CA 95053
408-554-4413

Santa Cruz

Venues

Catalyst
1011 Pacific Ave.
Santa Cruz, CA 95060
408-423-1338
Contact: Gary Tighe
P.O. Box 8545
Santa Cruz, CA 95061
408-425-7799

O.T. Prices
P.O. Box 487
Soquel, CA 95073
408-438-4025
Contact: Tom Miller

Record Stores

Cymbaline Records
435 Front Street
Santa Cruz, CA 95060
408-423-3949, 408-462-0600
Contact: Greg Penny or Ron
Prilliman

Logos Records
1117 Pacific Ave.
Santa Cruz, CA 95060
408-426-2106
Contact: Russell Potter

Universes Records
1214 A Pacific Ave.
Santa Cruz, CA 95060
408-425-1096
Indy Buyer

Radio Stations

KUSP
P.O. Box 423
Santa Cruz, CA 95061
408-476-2800

KZSC
University of California-Santa Cruz
Santa Cruz, CA 95064
408-429-2811

CALIFORNIA

Press

City on a Hill Press
The Stonehouse
University of California-Santa Cruz
Santa Cruz, CA 95064
408-429-4350
Contact: Harold Cecil, Music Editor

Good Times
P.O. Box 1885
Santa Cruz, CA 95061
408-426-8430
Contact: Richie Began

Santa Cruz Sentinel
P.O. Box 638
Santa Cruz, CA 95061
408-423-4242
Contact: Rick Chatnever

Sun
118 Union Street
Santa Cruz, CA 95060
408-429-8033
Contact: Michael Gant

Santa Monica

Venues

At My Place
1026 Wilshire Blvd.
Santa Monica, CA 90401
213-451-8596, 213-451-8597
Contact: Matt Krammer
Jazz, R & B, rock, and New Age

Madame Wong's
2900 West Wilshire Blvd.
Santa Monica, CA 90403
213-828-4444
Contact: Brian Smith
Pop rock

Record Stores

Off the Record
2621 Wilshire Blvd.
Santa Monica, CA 90403
213-829-7379
Contact: Jeff

Texas Records
712 Wilshire Blvd.
Santa Monica, CA 90401
213-392-5746
Contact: Michael Meister

Radio Stations

KCRW
1900 Pico Blvd.
Santa Monica, CA 90405
213-450-5183

Santa Rosa

Record Stores

Last Record Store
739 Fourth Street
Santa Rosa, CA 95404
707-525-1963
Contact: Doug Jayne or Hoit
Wilhielm

Radio Stations

KMLS/WATTZ
314 Gilbert, Suite 1
Santa Rosa, CA 95405
707-576-1997
Contact: Steve Wattz

31

KXFX
P.O. Box 2158
Santa Rosa, CA 95405
707-523-1369
Album-oriented station

Miscellaneous California

Venues

Old Town Bar
327 Second Street
Eureka, CA 95501
707-445-2971, X9711
Contact: Deborah

Safari Sam's
411 Olive Ave.
Huntington Beach, CA 92648
714-646-8706
Contact: Sam

Club, The
321 Alvarado
Monterey, CA 93940
408-646-9244
Booking agent: Gary Tighe
P.O. Box 8545
Santa Cruz, CA 95061
408-425-77992
Variety music

Happy Jack's Saloon
900 Main Street
Morro Bay, CA 93442
805-772-8478
Contact: Dave Tope
Rock 'n' roll

Vortex, The
260 California Ave.
Palo Alto, CA 94306
415-324-8443
Contact: General Manager
Variety music

Be-Bop
18433 Sherman Way
Receda, CA 91135
818-881-1654
Contact: Rich

Chatterbox
853 Valencia
Valencia, CA 94110
415-821-1891
Contact: Alfie
Rock 'n' roll

Record Stores

Tower Records
306 North Beach Blvd.
Anaheim, CA 92801
714-995-6600
Contact: Dennis

Small Town Records
7425 El Camino Real
Atascadero, CA 93422
805-461-9332
Contact: Barbara Simms

Tower Records
1160 B East Imperial Hgwy.
Brea, CA 92621
714-529-9996
Contact: Steve Unmack

Tower Records
7830 Macy Plaza Drive
Citrus Heights, CA 95610
916-961-7171
Contact: Phil Menas

Backdoor Records
8055 Old Redwood Hgwy.
Cotati, CA 94928
707-795-9597
Contact: Rick Warne

Blue Meanie Records
916 Broadway
El Cajon, CA 92021
619-442-5034
Contact: Mitch

Tower Records
796 Fletcher Pkwy.
El Cajon, CA 92020
619-579-9701
Contact: Maria Meiners or David
Berray

Down Home Music
10341 San Pablo Ave.
El Cerrito, CA 94530
415-525-1494
Contact: Frank Scott

Tower Records
23811 El Toro Road
El Toro, CA 92630
714-770-6242
Contact: Jim B.

Lou's Records
590 First Ave.
En Cinitas, CA 92024
619-753-1382
Indy Buyer

Sound Spectrum
1264 South Coast Hgwy.
Laguna Beach, CA 92651
714-494-5959
Contact: Jim Otto

Tower Records
630 San Antonio Road
Mount View, CA 94040
415-941-7900
Contact: Joe Zumba

Peer Records
2309 West Balboa Blvd.
Newport Beach, CA 92663
714-675-3752
Contact: Nick Adams

Watts Music
1211 Grant Ave.
Novato, CA 94945
415-897-2892
Contact: Ken Watts

Music Coop
271 North McDowell Blvd.
Petaluma, CA 94952
707-762-4257
Contact: John Brenes

Best Records
15023 Roscoe Blvd.
Panorama City, CA 91402
818-892-1475
Contact: Mark Rowe

Tower Records
8717 Van Nuys Blvd.
Panorama City, CA 91402
818-893-7808
Contact: Manuel Moreno

Maximum Music
555 Francisco Blvd.
San Rafael, CA 94901
415-454-9262
Contact: Tom Strange

Record Shop
2330 Marinship Way, Suite 207
Sausalito, CA 94965
415-331-7464
Indy Buyer
LP Buyer is: Jeff Loudon
Minneapolis, MN
612-545-2877

Tower Records
14612 Ventura Blvd.
Sherman Oaks, CA 91403
818-789-0500
Indy Buyer

Best Records
1263 Los Angeles Ave.
Simi Valley, CA 93063
805-527-8903
Contact: Jeff Joseph

Tower Records
6623 Pacific Ave.
Stockton, CA 95207
209-951-3700
Contact: Jeff Skoin

Important Records
20525 Manhattan Place
Torrance, CA 90501
213-212-0801
Contact: Marjorie Hines or Reed
Chaffey

Tower Records
22135 Hawthorne Blvd.
Torrance, CA 90503
213-316-4444
Contact: Chris Bryant

Wherehouse Entertainment
19701 Hamilton Ave.
Torrance, CA 90502-1311
213-538-2314
Indy Buyer

Tower Records
1205 West Covina Pkwy.
West Covina, CA 91790
818-962-8707
Contact: Steve Carrico

Radio Stations

KJAZ
1131 Harbor Bay Pkwy., Suite 200
Alameda, CA 94501
415-769-4800

KHSU
Humboldt State University
Arcata, CA 95521
707-826-4807

KROQ
3500 West Olive Ave., Suite 900
Burbank, CA 91505
818-567-1067

KOTR
840 Sheffield Road
Cambria, CA 93428
805-927-5021

KSPC
Pomona College
Thatcher Music Building
340 North College Ave.
Claremont, CA 91711
714-621-8157

KKUP
P.O. Box 820
Cupertino, CA 95015
408-253-0303

KDVS
University of California-Davis
14 Lower Freeborn Hall
Davis, CA 95616
916-752-0728

KBRG
39111 Paseo Padra Pkwy.
Fremont, CA 94538
415-791-1049

KFCR
Fullerton College
321 East Chapman Ave.
Fullerton, CA 92022
714-992-7264

KSDT
University of California-San Diego
UCSD/B-015
La Jolla, CA 92093
619-534-3673

KULV
University of La Verne
1950 Third Street
La Verne, CA 91750
714-596-1693

KFJC
Foothill College
12345 El Monte Road
Los Altos Hills, CA 94022
415-960-4260

KMBU
Peperdine University
Malibu, CA 90265
213-456-4022

KHYV
P.O. Box 3131
Modesto, CA 95353
209-523-7756

KSMC
St. Mary's College
P.O. Box 3223
Moraga, CA 94575
415-631-4252

KVMR
P.O. Box 1327
Nevada City, CA 95959
916-265-9073

Radio Chapman
Chapman College
333 North Glassell Street
Orange, CA 92666
714-997-6825

KAZU
P.O. Box 206
176 Forest Ave.
Pacific Grove, CA 93950
408-375-7275

KPCC
Pasadena City College
1570 East Colorado Blvd.
Pasadena, CA 91106
818-578-7231

KSPB
Robert L. Stevenson School
P.O. Box 657
Pebble Beach, CA 93953
408-624-1257, X336

KUOR
University of Redlands
1200 East Colton Ave.
Redlands, CA 92374
714-793-2121, X2830

KUCR
691 Linden
Riverside, CA 92507
714-787-3838

KSSB
California State University
5500 University Pkwy.
San Bernadino, CA 92407
714-887-7685

KKSM
Palomar College
San Marcos, CA 92069
619-744-1150, X5576

KCSB
University of California-Santa Barbara
UCEN, Room 3185A
Santa Barbara, CA 93106
805-961-3757

KTYD
5360 Hollifter Ave.
Santa Barbara, CA 93111
805-967-4511

KZSU
Stanford University
P.O. Box B
Stanford, CA 94305
415-725-4868

KRCL
California Lutheran College
60 West Wilson Road
Thousand Oaks, CA 91360
805-493-3470

KLLK
12 West Valley Street
Willits, CA 95490
707-459-1250

Press

Contrast Magazine
9348 Civic Center Drive, Suite 101
Beverly Hills, CA 90210
213-859-5766
Contact: Randy

No Answers
P.O. Box 680
University of California
Goleta, CA 93116
805-968-4340
Contact: Kent McClard

Sound Choice/Audio Evolution Network
P.O. Box 1251
Ojai, CA 93023
805-646-6814
Contact: David Ciaffardini

THE WEST

- [ ] Arizona
- [x] Colorado
- [x] Idaho
- [ ] Montana
- [x] Nevada
- [x] New Mexico
- [x] Oregon
- [x] Utah
- [x] Washington
- [x] Wyoming

A R I Z O N A

Tempe

Record Stores

East Side Records
217 West University
Tempe, AZ 85281
602-968-2011
Contact: Ben or Clayton

Tower Records
821 South Mill Ave.
Tempe, AZ 85281
602-968-7774
Contact: Ryan Preston or Indy Buyer

Radio Stations

KASR
Arizona State University
Stauffer Hall
Tempe, AZ 85287
602-965-4163

Tucson

Record Stores

WREX Records
1008 East Sixth Street
Tucson, AZ 85719
602-624-6252
Contact: Paul or Joe

Zip's Records
7091 East Speedway
Tucson, AZ 85710
602-747-0201
Contact: Rick Andrade

Radio Stations

KLPX
1920 West Copper
Tucson, AZ 85745
602-622-6711

KWFM
2100 North Silver Bell
Tucson, AZ 85745
602-623-7556

Press

Arizona Daily Star
P.O. Box 26807
Tucson, AZ 85726
602-573-4111
Contact: Scott Skinner

Citizen, The
P.O. Box 26767
Tucson, AZ 85726
602-573-4561
Contact: Chuck Graham

Wildcat
University of Arizona
Student Union, Room 4
Tucson, AZ 85721
602-621-3377

Miscellaneous Arizona

Venues

Monsoons
22 East Santa Fe
Flagstaff, AZ 86001
602-774-7929
Contact: Jake Horine

Record Stores

Tracks in Wax
4741 North Central Ave.
Phoenix, AZ 85012
602-274-2660
Contact: Dennis or Don

Tower Records
5617 North 19th Ave.
Phoenix, AZ 85015
602-246-7041
Contact: Craig Brown

Tower Records
3949 East Thomas Road
Phoenix, AZ 85018
602-273-1133
Contact: Richard Otter

Zia Records
1833 West Thunderbird Road
Phoenix, AZ 85023
602-866-7867
Contact: Maria Marshall

Radio Stations

KDKB
1167 West Javelina
Mesa, AZ 85210-5999
602-897-9300

KGRX
218 West Hampton Ave. #1
Mesa, AZ 85210
602-964-3100

KJZZ
1435 South Dobson Road
Mesa, AZ 85202
602-834-5627

C O L O R A D O

Boulder

Venues

T-Bird's Bar
2020 B. Tenth Street
Boulder, CO 80302
303-449-5787
Contact: Chase or Doug
Rock 'n' roll

Record Stores

Albums on the Hill
1128 13th Street
Boulder, CO 80302
303-447-0159
Contact: Lisa Lane or Andy Schneidkraut

Rocky Mountain Records
134 Pearl Street
Boulder, CO 80302
303-442-8750
Contact: Bob Zook

Trade a Tape and Records
1116 13th Street
Boulder, CO 80302
303-443-0636
Contact: Bill Moran or Indy Buyer

Radio Stations

KBCO
4801 Riverbend Road
Boulder, CO 80301
303-444-5600

KGNU
P.O. Box 885
Boulder, CO 80306
303-449-4885

KUCB
University of Colorado
P.O. Box 207
Boulder, CO 80309
303-492-5031

Colorado Springs

Record Stores

Budget Tapes and Record
327 North Tejon
Colorado Springs, CO 80903
719-471-4419
Contact: Leo Chance

Radio Stations

KEPC
C/O Pikes Peak Community College
5675 South Academy Blvd.
Colorado Springs, CO 08096
719-576-7711

KILO
707 South Pejon
Colorado Springs, CO 80903
719-634-4896

KRCC
Colorado College
117 East Cache La Poudre
Colorado Springs, CO 80903
719-473-4801

Denver

Denver is home to a lot of cover band clubs; original rock scene seems
to have died recently.

Venues

Parrish 23
2301 Blake Street
Denver, CO 80205
303-296-6628
Contact: Michael Lustig
New wave and progressive rock

Herman's Hideway
1578 South Broadway
Denver, CO 80210
303-778-9916
Contact: Allen Roth
Variety music

Metro
314 East 13th Ave.
Denver, CO 80218
303-839-5810
Contact: Lorin Karge
Dance music

Record Stores

Sound Warehouse
1235 East Evans Ave.
Denver, CO 80210
303-778-0320
LP Buyer

Wax Trax
638 East 13th Ave.
Denver, CO 80203
303-831-7246
Contact: Joe Beine

Radio Stations

KAOS
University of Denver
1770 South Williams
Denver, CO 80210
303-871-4405

KBPI Radio
17th Street, Suite 2300
Denver, CO 80202
303-572-6200

KCFR
2249 South Josephine Street
Denver, CO 80210
303-871-9191

KVOD
1601 West Jewel Ave.
Denver, CO 80223
303-936-3428

Press

Westword
P.O. Box 5970
2401 15th Street, Suite 220
Denver, CO 80217
303-458-6616
Contact: Gil Asakawa

Fort Collins

Venues

Fort Ram
450 North Linden
Fort Collins, CO 80524
303-482-5026
Contact: Mike Ledbetter
Dance rock

Record Stores

Front Range Records
632 South College Ave.
Fort Collins, CO 80521
303-493-6420
Contact: Dave

Radio Stations

KCSU
Lory Student Center
Colorado State University
Fort Collins, CO 80523
303-491-7611/2

KTCL
P.O. Box 2047
Fort Collins, CO 80522
303-493-5330

Miscellaneous Colorado

Venues

Little Bear, The
P.O. Box 1366
Evergreen, CO 80439
303-674-9991, 303-697-5669
Contact: John Lamana
Rock 'n' roll and R & B

Record Stores

Recycle Records
6739 West Colfax
Lakewood, CO 80215
303-238-4289
Contact: Jerry or Bill

Radio Stations

KASF
Adams State College
110 Richardson Ave.
Alamosa, CO 81101
719-589-7154

KSPN
305 L Aspen Airport Business Center
Aspen, CO 81611
303-925-5776

KBUT
P.O. Box 38
Crested Butte, CO 81224
303-349-7444

KDUR
Fort Lewis College
P.O. Box 339
Durango, CO 81302
303-247-7262

KMSA
Mesa College
1175 Texas Ave.
Grand Junction, CO 81502
303-248-1240

KVNF
213 Grand Ave.
P.O. Box 538
Paonia, CO 81428
303-527-4866

KFMU
P.O. Box 772850
Steamboat Springs, CO 80477
303-879-5368

KSBT and KBCR
P.O. Box 774050
Steamboat Springs, CO 80477
303-879-2270

I D A H O

Boise

Record Stores

5 Mile Records
10366 Overland Road
Boise, ID 83709
208-377-8496
Contact: Rick Simmons

Budget Records
1225 Broadway Ave.
Boise, ID 83706
208-336-4122
Contact: Michael Bunnell or Matt Anderson

Record Exchange
1105 West Idaho
Boise, ID 83702
208-344-8010
Contact: Liam Elms

Spike's Records and CD's
413 South Eighth Street
Boise, ID 83702
208-343-4481
Contact: Spike

Radio Stations

KBSU
Boise State University
1910 University Drive
Boise, ID 83725
208-385-3663

Miscellaneous Idaho

Radio Stations

KUOI
University of Idaho
Student Union Building
Moscow, ID 83843
208-885-6433

M O N T A N A

Bozeman

Record Stores

Cactus Records
29 West Main Street
Bozeman, MT 59715
406-587-0245
Contact: Barb Allen

Radio Stations

KGLT
Montana State University
Strand Union Building, Room 325
Bozeman, MT 59717
406-994-3001

N E V A D A

Las Vegas

Record Stores

Tower Records
4700 South Maryland Pkwy.
Las Vegas, NV 89119
702-798-6800
Contact: Suzy Kormanik

Underground Records
1164 East Twain Ave.
Las Vegas, NV 89109
702-733-7025
Contact: Wayne Coyner

Radio Stations

KEYV
66 East Tropicana Ave.
Las Vegas, NV 89109
702-736-9393

KNPR
5151 Boulder Hgwy.
Las Vegas, NV 89122
702-456-6695

KUNV-UNLV
4505 Maryland Pkwy.
Las Vegas, NV 89154
702-739-3877

N E W   M E X I C O

Albuquerque

Record Stores

Bow Wow Records
3103 Central Ave. Northeast
Albuquerque, NM 87106
505-256-0928
Indy Buyer

KUNM
University of New Mexico
Onate Hall
Albuquerque, NM 87131
505-277-4806

Radio Stations

KHFM
5900 Domingo Road Northeast
Albuquerque, NM 87108
505-262-2631

Santa Fe

Venues

Club West
213 West Alameda
Santa Fe, NM 87501
505-982-4523
Contact: Allan Hoffman

Music Shop, The
1722 D St. Michaels Drive
Santa Fe, NM 87505
505-471-2833
Contact: Adele

Record Stores

Candyman Center, The
851 St. Michaels Drive
Santa Fe, NM 87504
505-983-9309
Indy Buyer

Rare Bear Records
1303 Cerrillos Road
Santa Fe, NM 87501
505-988-3531
Contact: James Albright

Miscellaneous New Mexico

Radio Stations

KNMS
Dept. CC
P.O. Box 30001
New Mexico State University
Las Cruces, NM 88003-0001
505-646-4640

KTAO
P.O. Box 1844
Taos, NM 87571
505-758-1017

O R E G O N

Corvallis

Record Stores

Audio Addict
1561 Northwest Monroe Ave.
Corvallis, OR 97330
503-758-7433
Indy Buyer

Happy Trails Records
133 Southwest Second Street
Corvallis, OR 97333
503-752-9032
Contact: Doug or Dave

Radio Stations

KBVR
Oregon State University
Snell Hall
Corvallis, OR 97331-1619
503-754-2008

Eugene

Venues

Cultural Forum
Erb Memorial Union, Suite 2
University of Oregon
Eugene, OR 97403
503-686-4373
Contact: Frank Byers or Jerry Dixon

Record Stores

Record Garden
957 Willamette
Eugene, OR 97401
503-344-7625
Contact: Mike McAdams

Radio Stations

KRVM
200 North Monroe Street
Eugene, OR 97402
503-687-3370

KZAM
P.O. Box 1123
Eugene, OR 97440
503-741-1999

KZEL
2100 West 11th Ave.
Eugene, OR 97402
503-342-7096

La Grande

Record Stores

La Grande Stereo and Music
111 North First Street
La Grande, OR 97850
503-963-5933
Contact: Mike Malory

Radio Stations

KEOL
East Oregon State College
Walter M. Pierce Library
La Grande, OR 97850
503-963-1397

Portland

Venues

Pine Street
221 Southeast Ninth Ave.
Portland, OR 97214
503-235-0027
Variety music

Satericon
125 Northwest Sixth Ave.
Portland, OR 97209
503-243-2380
Contact: George

Starry Night
8 Northwest Seventh Ave.
Portland, OR 97209
503-227-0069
Contact: Larry

Record Stores

2nd Avenue Records
418 Southwest Second Ave.
Portland, OR 97204
503-222-3783
Contact: John McNally

Budget Tapes and Records
631 Southwest Alder
Portland, OR 97205
503-226-0624
Contact: Jacque Goldstone

Everybody's Records
5279 North Lombard Street
Portland, OR 97203
503-286-9841
Contact: Jeff Farnadad

Music Millenium
3158 East Burnside
Portland, OR 97214
503-231-8943
Contact: Terry Currier

Ooze Records, The
2190 West Burnside Street
Portland, OR 97210
503-226-0249
Contact: Charles Powne

Rockport Records
203 Southwest Ninth
Portland, OR 97205
503-224-0660
Contact: Dave Clingan

Tower Records
4100 Southeast 82nd Ave.
Portland, OR 97266
503-777-8460
Contact: Kim Cretsinger

Radio Stations

KBOO
20 Southeast Eighth
Portland, OR 97213
503-231-8032

KINK
1501 Southwest Jefferson
Portland, OR 97201
503-226-5080

KLCC
Lewis and Clark College
P.O. Box 59
Portland, OR 97219
503-244-6161

KRRC
Reed College
3203 Southeast Woodstock Blvd.
Portland, OR 97202
503-771-1112, X391

Press

Willamette Week
2 Northwest Second Ave.
Portland, OR 97209
503-243-2122
Contact: Kip Richardson

Miscellaneous Oregon

Record Stores

Diana's Records
343 East Main
Ashland, OR 97520
503-488-0066
Contact: Fred Murschall

Rare Earth Records
37 North Main
Ashland, OR 97520
503-482-9501
Contact: Jason Moore

Tower Records
3175 Southwest Cedar Hills Blvd.
Beaverton, OR 97005
503-626-2600
Contact: Dave Williams

Larson's Stereo Den
P.O. Box 1748
Medford, OR 97501
503-779-3211
Contact: Mark Doern

Radio Stations
KTEC
Oregon Institute Of Technology
Klamath Falls, OR 97601
503-882-1776

KSLC
Linfield College
700 South Baker
McMinnville, OR 97128
503-472-3851

U T A H

Salt Lake City

Venues

Zephyr
P.O. Box 2540
301 Southwest Temple
Salt Lake City, UT 84110
801-355-2582
Contact: Sam Callis
Variety music

Record Stores

Cosmic Aeroplane Books
258 East First Street
Salt Lake City, UT 84111
801-533-9409
Contact: Doug Stalker
New Age tapes

Smokey's Records
1515 South 1500 East
Salt Lake City, UT 84105
801-486-8709
Contact: Smokey Koelsch

Radio Stations
KRPN
5065 West 2100 South
Salt Lake City,UT 84120
801-972-3449

KUER
University of Utah
103 Kingsbury Hall
Salt Lake City, UT 84112
801-581-6625

Miscellaneous Utah

Radio Stations

KWCR
Weber State College
3750 Harrison Blvd.
Ogden, UT 84408
801-626-6450

KPCW
P.O. Box 1372
Park City, UT 84060
801-649-9004

WASHINGTON

Bellevue

Record Stores

Tower Records
10635 Northeast Eighth Street
Bellevue, WA 98409
206-451-2557
Contact: Terry Day

Radio Stations

KBCS
Bellevue Community College
3000 Landerholm Circle Southeast
Bellevue, WA 98007
206-641-2424

Bellingham

Record Stores

Budget Tapes and Records
1330 Railroad Ave.
Bellingham, WA 98225
206-676-9573
Contact: Gil

Cellophane Square Records
1331-A Cornwall Ave.
Bellingham, WA 98225
206-676-1404, 206-634-2280
Contact: Steve

Golden Oldies Records
2000 North State Street
Bellingham, WA 98225
206-671-8907
Contact: Chuck Foster

Landing Discs and Tapes
1307 11th Street
Bellingham, WA 98225
206-647-1307
Contact: Tom Barnard

Zephyr Records
114 East Magnolia
Bellingham, WA 98225
206-671-1077
Contact: Bob Staples

Radio Stations

KUGS
Western Washington State College
410 Viking Union
Bellingham, WA 98225
206-676-5847

Olympia

Record Stores

Positively 4th Street
208 West Fourth Ave.
Olympia, WA 98501
206-786-8273
Contact: Win Vidor

Rainy Day Records
Westside Center Y
Olympia, WA 98502
206-357-4755
Contact: Dave Baxter

Radio Stations

KAOS
Evergreen State College
Cab 305
Olympia, WA 98505
206-866-6822

Seattle

Venues

Backstage
2208 Northwest Market Street
Seattle, WA 98107
206-789-1184
Contact: Ed Breeson
Variety music

Central Tavern
2537 Second West
Seattle, WA 98107
206-622-0209
Contact: Terry

Record Stores

Cellophane Square Record Store
1315 Northeast 42nd Street
Seattle, WA 98105
206-634-2280
Contact: Steve Marcus

Discount Records
4530 University Way Northeast
Seattle, WA 98105
206-633-3023
Contact: Thomas

Easy Street Records
4537 California Ave. Southwest
Seattle, WA 98116
206-932-5693
Contact: Larry Nixon

Fallout Records
1506 East Olive Way
Seattle, WA 98122
206-323-2662
Contact: Janet Johnson

Orpheum Records
618 Broadway East
Seattle, WA 98102
206-322-6370
Contact: Bruce Bonifaci

Park Avenue Records
532 Queen Anne Ave. North
Seattle, WA 98109
206-284-2390
Contact: Bob Jenniker

Time Travelers Records
1511 Second Ave.
Seattle, WA 98101
206-624-7806
Contact: David Lamb

Tower Records
500 Mercer Street
Seattle, WA 98109
206-283-4456
Contact: Cindy Chin

Tower Records
4321 University Way Northeast
Seattle, WA 98105
206-632-1187
Contact: Jim Portnick

Radio Stations

KCMU
University of Washington
Seattle, WA 98195
206-543-4680

KEZX
3876 Bridgeway North
Seattle, WA 98103
206-633-5590

KISW
712 Aurora Ave. North
Seattle, WA 98109
206-285-7625

KUOW
University of Washington
Seattle, WA 98195
206-543-9595

KXRX
3131 Elliott Ave., Seventh Floor
Seattle, WA 98121
206-283-5979

KZOK
200 West Mercer, Suite 304
Seattle, WA 98119
206-281-5600

Press

Rocket Magazine Monthly
2028 Fifth Ave.
Seattle, WA 98121
206-728-7625
Contact: Charles Cross

Tacoma

Record Stores

Tower Records
2501 South 38th Street
Tacoma, WA 98409
206-475-9222
Contact: Steve White

Radio Stations

KUPS
University of Puget Sound
1500 North Warner
Tacoma, WA 98416
206-756-3277

Miscellaneous Washington

Radio Stations

KGRG
12401 Southeast 120th Street
Auburn, WA 98002
206-833-5004

KXLE
1311 Vantage Hgwy.
Ellensburg, WA 98926
509-925-1488

KSVR
Skagit Valley College
2405 College Way
Mount Vernon, WA 98273
206-428-1186

KUGR
Washington State University
Murrow Communications Center,
Room 301
Pullman, WA 99163-2530
509-335-5042

KZUU
Washington State University
Compton Union, Third Floor
Pullman, WA 99164-7204
509-335-2208

KKZX
South 5106 Palouse Hgwy.
Spokane, WA 99223
509-448-9900

KWRS
Whitworth College
Spokane, WA 99251
509-466-3278

KWCW
Whitman College
Student Union Building
Walla Walla, WA 99362
509-527-5283

KSSY
1022 North Wenatchee
Wenatchee, WA 98801
509-663-5186

KATS
114 South Fourth
Yakima, WA 98901
509-457-8117

Press

Victory Music Review
P.O. Box 7515
Bonney Lake Drive
Sumner, WA 98390
206-863-6617
Contact: Chris Lunn
Monthly fanzine

W Y O M I N G

Miscellaneous Wyoming
Radio Stations

KTAG
P.O. Box 893
2001 Mountainview
Cody, WY 82414
307-587-2211

KRQU
409 South Fourth
Laramie, WY 82070
307-742-1029

KUWR
University of Wyoming
P.O. Box 3984
Laramie, WY 82071
307-766-6624

KCWC
Central Wyoming College
2660 Peck Ave.
Riverton, WY 82501
307-856-4441

MID - AMERICA

- Iowa
- Kansas
- Missouri
- Nebraska
- North Dakota
- Oklahoma
- South Dakota
- Texas

I O W A

Ames

There are some things happening here.

Venues

Maintenance Shop, The
Memorial Union, Room 35
Ames, IA 50011
515-294-2758
Contact: Mike Reilly

Record Stores

Music Works
127 Welch Street
Ames, IA 50010
515-292-1919
Contact: Paul Miller

Radio Stations

KUSR
Iowa State University
1199 Friley Hall
Ames, IA 50012
515-294-4332

Cedar Falls

Venues

Steb's
2215 College Street
Cedar Falls, IA 50613
319-277-0071
Contact: Sherm McNeil

Record Stores

Omni Records
2222 College Street
Cedar Falls, IA 50613
319-277-7360
Contact: Tim or Candy

Radio Stations

KCRS
University of Northern Iowa
Maucker Union
Cedar Falls, IA 50614
319-273-6935

KUNI
University of Northern Iowa
Broadcasting Services
Cedar Falls, IA 50614-0359
319-273-6400
Contact: Carl Jenkins

Iowa City

Venues

Gabe's Oasis
330 East Washington
Iowa City, IA 52240
319-354-4788
Contact: Doug Roberson
Blues, alternative rock, jazz, and reggae

Record Stores

BJ's Records
6½ South Dubuque Street
Iowa City, IA 52240
319-338-8251
Contact: Greg Leanhart

Record Collector
4½ South Linn Street
Iowa City, IA 52240
319-337-5029
Contact: Kirk Walther

Radio Stations

KRUI
University of Iowa
897 South Quad
Iowa City, IA 52242
319-335-9525
Contact: Sara Didonato, Program Director

KSUI
University of Iowa
3300 Engineering Building
Iowa, City, IA 52242
319-335-5730
Contact: John Fischer, Program Director

Miscellaneous Iowa

Record Stores

Co-op Records
422 East Locust
Davenport, IA 52802
319-324-8522
Contact: Scott

Radio Stations

KBLE
1170 22nd Street
P.O. Box 1143
Des Moines, IA 50311
515-288-3033
Contact: Ron Sorenson, Program Director

KDIC
Grinnell College
P.O. Box V4
Grinnell, IA 50112
515-269-3335

KFMH
3218 Mulberry Ave.
Muscatine, IA 52761
319-263-2442
Contact: Steve Bridges, Program Director

KRNL
Cornell College
Mount Vernon, IA 52314
319-895-4432

KSEZ/FM
P.O. Box 177
Sioux City, IA 51102
712-258-6740
Contact: Tim Harrison, Program Director

K A N S A S

Lawrence

College community; great town for music.

Venues

Bottleneck
737 New Hampshire Street
Lawrence, KS 66044
913-843-9723
Contact: Brett Mosiman

Jazz Haus
926½ Massachusetts Street
Lawrence, KS 66044
913-749-3320
Contact: Rick McNeely

Radio Stations

KJHK
Blake Annex
University of Kansas
200 Stauffer-Flint
Lawrence, KS 66045
913-864-4745

Wichita

Venues

Coyote Club
3813 North Broadway
Wichita, KS 67219
316-838-9805
Contact: Art Busch

Record Stores

Music Incorporated
3203 East Douglas
Wichita, KS 67218
316-681-2025
Contact: Bill Snyder

Radio Stations

KMUW
Wichita State University
3317 East 17th
Wichita, KS 67208
316-682-5737

Miscellaneous Kansas

Record Stores

Streetside Records
9524 Antioch
Overland Park, KS 66214
913-381-2676
Contact: Kurt Wegner

Radio Stations

KXTR
1701 South 55th Street
Kansas City, KS 66106
913-432-1480
Contact: Rob Howig, Program Director

KSDB
Kansas State University
Kedzie Hall
Manhattan, KS 66506
913-532-3292

KKOW
Route 5
P.O. Box 45
Pittsburg, KS 66762
316-231-7200
Contact: Jeff Freeman, Program
Director

MISSOURI

Columbia
Venues

Blue
910 Business Loop, 70E
Columbia, MO 65205
314-874-1944
Contact: Richard King
Progressive, blues, reggae and rock 'n'
roll

Record Stores

Discount Records
806 A East Broadway
Columbia, MO 65201
314-442-2598
Contact: Laurie Astroth

Streetside Records
222 East Broadway
Columbia, MO 65201
314-875-7105
Contact: Kevin Walsh

Whizz Records
802 Conley Ave.
Columbia, MO 65201
314-443-1222
Indy Buyer

Radio Stations

KCOU
University of Missouri-Columbia
101-F Pershing Hall
Columbia, MO 65201
314-882-7820

KWWC
Stephens College
P.O. Box 2114
Columbia, MO 65215
314-876-7297

Kansas City
Venues

Grand Emporium
3832 Main Street
Kansas City, MO 64111
816-531-7557
Contact: Roger or Charlie

Record Stores

Penny Lane Records
4128 Broadway
Kansas City, MO 64111
816-561-1580
Indy Buyer

Seventh Heaven Records
7621 Troost Ave.
Kansas City, MO 64131
816-361-9555
Contact: Richard Klecka or Daryl
Housh

Streetside Records
556 Westport Road
Kansas City, MO 64111
816-561-9960
Contact: Manager

Press

K.C. Star
1729 Grand Ave.
Kansas City, MO 64108
816-234-4141
Contact: Evie Rapport,
Entertainment Editor
Mid American Daily

St. Louis

Venues

Blueberry Hill
6504 Delmar
St. Louis, MO 63130
314-727-0880
Contact: Bruce Homeyer

Mississippi Nights
914 North First Street
St. Louis, MO 63102
314-421-3853
Contact: Pat Hagin

Record Stores

Euclid Records
4906 Laclede Ave.
St. Louis, MO 63108
314-361-7353
Contact: Tony Margerita or Joe
Schwab

Streetside Records
2055 Walton Road
St. Louis, MO 63114
314-426-2388
Contact: Greg Marshall

Vintage Vinyl
6362 Delmar Blvd.
St. Louis, MO 63130
314-721-8746 or 314-721-4096
Contact: Steve Pick

West End Wax
389 North Euclid
St. Louis, MO 63108
314-367-0111
Contact: Debbie Mikles

Radio Stations

KDHX
3504 Magnolia
St. Louis, MO 63118
314-664-3955

KWMU
University of Missouri
8001 Natural Bridge Road
St. Louis, MO 63121
314-553-5488

KWUR
P.O. Box 1182
Washington University
Lindell & Skinker Blvd.
St. Louis, MO 63130
314-889-5952

Press

Jet Lag
8419 Halls Ferry Road
St. Louis, MO 63147-1893
314-383-5841
Monthly fanzine

River Front Times
1221 Locust Street, Suite 900
St. Louis, MO 63103
314-231-6666
Contact: Terry Perkins, Music Editor

Miscellaneous Missouri

Venues

Regency
307 Park Central
Springfield, MO 65806
417-862-2700
Contact: Gary Thomas

Record Stores

Streetside Records
742 North New Ballas Road
Creve Coeur, MO 63141
314-432-1153
Indy Buyer

Streetside Records
7927 North Linburg
Hazelwood, MO 63042
314-838-0522
Contact: Randy

Streetside Records
3609 B Noland Road
Independence, MO 64055
816-252-4250
Contact: Manager

Streetside Records
6314 Delmar Blvd.
University City, MO 63130
314-726-6277
Indy Buyer

Streetside Records
34 South Old Orchard Road
Webster Groves, MO 63119
314-961-7008

Radio Stations

KCFV
St. Louis Community College
3400 Pershall Road
Ferguson, MO 63135
314-595-4478
Contact: Jerry Persha, Program
Director

KXCV
Northwest Missouri State University
Wellf Hall
Maryville, MO 64468
816-562-1163
Contact: Sharon Carter, Program
Director

KMNR
210 HSS Building
Rolla, MO 65401
314-341-4272
Contact: Dave Merriwether,
Program Director

KCLC
Lindenwood College
St. Charles, MO 63301
314-946-2762
Contact: Rich Reighard

N E B R A S K A

Lincoln

Record Stores

Twisters
1401 O Street
Lincoln, NE 68508
402-477-6061
Indy Buyer

Radio Stations

KFMQ
1540 South 70th Street, Suite 200
Lincoln, NE 68506
402-489-6500
Contact: Brent Albert, Program
Director

KZUM
941 O Street
Lincoln, NE 68508
402-474-5086

Omaha

Venues

Howard Street Station
1112 Howard Street
Omaha, NE 68102
402-341-0433
Contact: Rick Renn
Blues, reggae, and alternative rock

Record Stores

Mr. Doug Records
P.O. Box 44011
15561 Hickory
Omaha, NE 68144
402-333-5839
Contact: Doug

Pickles Records
13830 T Plaza
Omaha, NE 68137
402-896-0218
Contact: Grant

Radio Stations

KIOS
3230 Burt Street
Omaha, NE 68131
402-554-6444
Contact: Bob Coate, Program
Director

KRCK
5010 Dodge Street
Omaha, NE 68132
402-553-0980

Miscellaneous Nebraska

Record Stores

Budget Tapes
1522 Broadway
Scottsbluff, NE 69361
308-635-1044
Contact: John Sylvester

N O R T H   D A K O T A

Fargo

Record Stores

Budget Records
4015 13th Ave. South
Fargo, ND 58103
701-282-0673
Contact: Calvin

Radio Stations

KQWB
P.O. Box 1301
Fargo, ND 58107
218-236-7900

Miscellaneous North Dakota

Radio Stations

KCND
1814 North 15th Street
Bismarck, ND 58501
701-224-1700
Contact: Roger Lockbeam, Program
Director

KNOX
P.O. Box 1638
Grand Forks, ND 58206
701-775-4611
Contact: Dave Salo, Program
Director

O K L A H O M A

Norman

Record Stores

Shadow Play Records
773 Asp Street
Norman, OK 73069
405-364-1670
Contact: Ruth

Radio Stations

KGOU
780 Van Vleet Oval
Norman, OK 73019
405-325-3388
Contact: Steve Patrick, Program
Director

Tulsa

Venues

Sunset Grill
2217 East Skelly Drive
Tulsa, OK 74105
918-744-5550
Contact: Bill

Radio Stations

KWGS
600 South College Ave.
Tulsa, OK 74104
918-592-5947
Contact: Edward Dumit, Program
Director

Miscellaneous Oklahoma

Record Stores

Wilcox Records
5517 North Penn
Oklahoma City, OK 73112
405-843-0900
Contact: Frank

Radio Stations

KHIB
Southeastern State University
P.O. Box 4129
Station A
Durant, OK 74701
405-924-0149

KVRO
Oklahoma State University
217½ South Washington
Stillwater, OK 74074
405-372-6000
Contact: Dave Collins, Program
Director

S O U T H   D A K O T A

Rapid City

Record Stores

Ernie November Records
1028 East North Street
Rapid City, SD 57701
605-341-0768
Contact: Roger

Radio Stations

KTEQ
South Dakota School of Mines
500 East St. Joe
Rapid City, SD 57701
605-394-2231

Miscellaneous South Dakota
Radio Stations

KGKG
P.O. Box 97
Brookings, SD 57006
605-692-1430
Contact: Brian Curtis, Program
Director

KAUR
Augustana College
Sioux Falls, SD 57197
605-336-5463

KRSD
Augustana College
P.O. Box 737
Sioux Falls, SD 57197
605-335-6666

KBHU
Black Hills State
P.O. Box 9665
1200 University Ave.
Spearfish, SD 57783
605-642-6737

KAOR
414 East Clark Street
University of South Dakota
Vermillion, SD 57069
605-677-5049

KUSD
414 East Clark Street
Vermillion, SD 57069
605-677-5861

T E X A S

Amarillo
Record Stores

Hasting's Books and Records
45th Street Southwest
Amarillo, TX 79103
806-359-5321
Indy Buyer

Sound Warehouse
2003 South Georgia
Amarillo, TX 79109
806-358-1376
Contact: Brad Clark

Radio Stations

KACV
Amarillo Junior College
P.O. Box 447
Amarillo, TX 79178
806-371-5227

KHWK
P.O. Box 30,000
Amarillo, TX 79120
806-374-1071

Arlington
Venues

J. Gilligans
407 East South Street
Arlington, TX 76010
817-274-8561
Contact: Dan Sinet

Press

UTA Shorthorn
P.O. Box 19038
Arlington, TX 76019
817-273-3784
Contact: Greg Bischof, Music Editor

Austin

Clubs here are changing faster than the telephone company can list their phone numbers.

Venues

Club Cairo
306 East Sixth Street
Austin, TX 78701
512-472-2476
Contact: Brad

Continental Club
P.O. Box 3843
Austin, TX 78764
512-441-2444
Contact: Wayne Nagel
Blues

Liberty Lunch
Guadalupe and Second Street
Austin, TX
512-477-0461
Contact: Mark Pratz

Opera House
200 Academy Drive
Austin, TX 78704
512-443-8885
Contact: David Mabry

Record Stores

Take advantage of Austin's plethora of record stores.
Austin Record Distribution
P.O. Box 312
Austin, TX 78767
512-451-9770
Contact: Susan Jarrott

Harmony House
8620 Burnet Road, Suite 101
Austin, TX 78758
512-339-1155, 512-452-4500
Contact: Jim

Inner Sanctum Records
504 West 24th Street
Austin, TX 78705
512-472-9459
Contact: Patrick Helton

Sound Exchange
2100 A Guadalupe
Austin, TX 78705
512-476-8742
Contact: Ryan Walker

Sound Warehouse
4901 Burnet Road
Austin, TX 78756
512-458-5253
Contact: Pete Salinas

Sound Warehouse
4301 Manchaca
Austin, TX 78704
512-443-7997
Contact: Luanne Williams

Sound Warehouse
1014 North Lamar Blvd.
Castle Hill Plaza, Suite A
Austin, TX 78703
512-479-8422
LP Buyer

Waterloo Records
221 South Lamar Blvd.
Austin, TX 78704
512-479-0473
Contact: Don Lamb

Radio Stations

KLBJ
P.O. Box 610310
Austin, TX 78761-0310
512-832-4000

KMFA
3001 North Lamar, Suite 100
Austin, TX 78705
512-476-5632

KPEZ
3001 Lake Austin Blvd., #400
Austin, TX 78703
512-478-6900

KUT
University of Texas
Communications Building B
Austin, TX 78712
512-471-6395

Press

Austin Chronicle
P.O. Box 49066
Austin, TX 78765
512-473-8995
Contact: Louis Block

Texas Monthly
P.O. Box 1569
Austin, TX 78767
512-476-7085
Contact: Joe Nick Patowski

College Station

Record Stores

Hastings Records
1631 Texas Ave.
College Station, TX 77840
409-693-7781
Contact: Bill Compere

Music Express
1725 B University Drive
College Station, TX 77840
409-846-1741
Contact: Jay

Radio Stations

KANM
Texas A & M
P.O. Box 377
College Station, TX 77841
409-845-5923

Dallas

A smart stop in Texas in terms of making money, but the crowds are difficult to please. The local scene seems to be developing.

Venues

500 Cafe
408 Exposition Ave.
Dallas, TX 75226
214-821-4623
Contact: Diane or Brian

Club Clearview
2806 Elm Street
Dallas, TX 75226
214-939-0006
Contact: Robin Welker
2801 Main Street
Dallas, TX 75226
Original music

Club Dada
2720 Elm Street
Dallas, TX 75226
214-744-3232
Contact: Doak Boettinger
All kinds of original music

Dallas Alley
2019 North Lamar, Suite 200
Dallas, TX 75202
214-720-0170
Contact: Jerry Thompson

Hard Rock Cafe
2601 McKinney
Dallas, TX 75201
214-855-5115
Contact: Tony Pace

Long Horn, The
216 Corinth
Dallas, TX 75207
214-428-3128
Contact: Wilson Wren

On the Rocks
2612 Commerce
Dallas, TX 75226
214-747-3637
Contact: Marcus Richmond
Heavy metal

Poor David's Pub
1924 Greenville Ave.
Dallas, TX 75206
214-821-9891
Contact: David Card

Starck Club
703 McKinney
Dallas, TX 75202
214-720-0130
Contact: Greg McCone

Record Stores

Big State Distribution
4830 Lakawana, Suite #121
Dallas, TX 75247
214-631-1100
Contact: Ellen Magid

Bill's Records
8136 Spring Valley Road
Dallas, TX 75240
214-234-1496
Contact: Bill Weisner

Collector's Records
10616 Garland Road
Dallas, TX 75218
214-327-3313
Contact: Dorothy

Half-Price Bookstores
5915 East Northwest Hgwy.
Dallas, TX 75231
214-363-8374
Contact: Steve Leach

Hit Records
2402 Gus Thomasson Road
Dallas, TX 75228
214-324-1927
Contact: Ron Ross

Record Gallery
1921½ Greenville Ave.
Dallas, TX 75206
214-824-2201
Contact: Steven Stokes

Recycled Records
9020 Garland Road
Dallas, TX 75218
214-321-3571
Contact: Paul White

Sound Warehouse
5425 Greenville Ave.
Dallas, TX 75206
214-692-9750
Contact: Mark Christie

VVV Records
3906 Cedar Springs
Dallas, TX 75219
214-522-3470
Contact: Neil Caldwell

Radio Stations

KERA
3000 Harry Hines Blvd.
Dallas, TX 75201
214-871-1390

KNON
P.O. Box 710909
Dallas, TX 75371
214-828-9500

KSMU
Southern Methodist University
P.O. Box 456
Dallas, TX 75275
214-692-4525

KZEW
3625 North Hall, Suite Penthouse 100
Dallas, TX 75219
214-522-9898

Press

72 Hours
P.O. Box 134
Southern Methodist-Student Media
Dallas, TX 75275
214-692-2000
Contact: Katherine Blackmon, Music Editor

Buddy
501 North Good-Latimer Expressway
Dallas, TX 75204
214-826-8742
Contact: Stoney Burns

Dallas Morning News
508 Young Street
Dallas, TX 75202
214-977-8408
Contact: Ken Perkins

Dallas Observer
2330 Butler Street, Suite 115
Dallas, TX 75235
214-637-2072
Contact: Clay McNear

Dallas Times Herald
1101 Pacific Ave.
Dallas, TX 75202
214-720-6111
Contact: Bob Brock, Entertainment

Detour
3100 Carlisle, Suite 219
Dallas, TX 75204
214-969-0355
Contact: David Feld, Editor

Denton

Venues

Library, The
1210 West Hickory
Denton, TX 75201
817-566-2199
Contact: Jim Lott

Press

North Texas Daily
P.O. Box 5278
North Texas Station
Denton, TX 76203
817-565-2353

Fort Worth

Venues

Caravan of Dreams
312 Houston Street
Fort Worth, TX 76102
817-429-4000
Contact: Maria Golia
Jazz

Hop, The
2905 West Berry
Fort Worth, TX 76109
817-923-7281
Contact: Mark Benedict

J & J Blues Bar
937 Woodward
Fort Worth, TX 76102
817-870-2337
Contact: Phil Merrit

Joe's Garage
9502 Hgwy. 80 West
Fort Worth, TX 76116
817-244-4456

West Side Stories
3900 Hgwy. #377 South
Fort Worth, TX 76116
817-560-7632
Contact: Gary Osier

Record Stores

Record Town
3025 South University Drive
Fort Worth, TX 76109
817-926-1331
Indy Buyer

Sound Warehouse
6393 Camp Bowie Blvd.
Fort Worth, TX 76116
817-737-8831
Contact: Charles Buxton

Press

Performance
1203 Lake Street, Suite 200
Fort Worth, TX 76102-4504
817-338-9444
Contact: Louis Marrogun, Managing Editor
International touring talent weekly news

Houston

"I've seen many groups develop and start their careers here."
—Mark Bouman, independent writer

Venues

Fitzgerald's
2706 White Oak
Houston, TX 77007
713-862-8452, 713-862-3838
Contact: Melissa Cherry

Rockefellers
3620 Washington Ave.
Houston, TX 77007
713-861-8925
Contact: Colleen Fisher or Don Gomez

Record Stores

Cactus Records
2930 South Shepard Drive
Houston, TX 77098
713-526-9272
Contact: Debbie Brown

Infinite Records
528 Westheimer
Houston, TX 77006
713-521-0187
Contact: Dave Ritz

Marcus Garvey Records
4635 Belfort Ave.
Houston, TX 77051
713-734-3565
Contact: Stephen James

Record Exchange
1718 Westheimer
Houston, TX 77098
713-666-5555
Contact: Kurt

Record Rack
3109 South Shepard
Houston, TX 77098
713-524-3602
Contact: Bruce Godwin

Sound Warehouse
3800 Farnham
Houston, TX 77098
713-523-2200

Sound Warehouse
6520 Westheimer
Houston, TX 77057
713-977-0001
Contact: Gary Moore

Tapes and T's
8409 Hillcroft
Houston, TX 77096
713-541-2919
Contact: Todd Davis

Radio Stations

KLOL-FM
510 Lovett Blvd.
Houston, TX 77006
713-526-6855

KPFT
419 Lovett Blvd.
Houston, TX 77006
713-526-4000

KRTS
1010 Lamar, Suite 1320
Houston, TX 77002
713-228-9292

KTRU
Rice University
P.O. Box 1892
Houston, TX 77251
713-527-4098

KTSU
Texas Southern University
3100 Cleburne
Houston, TX 77004
713-527-7591

Press

Cool Runnings
P.O. Box 740334
Houston, TX 77274-0334
713-271-2742
Contact: Kathy Todd, Publisher
Monthly fanzine

Public News
1540 West Alabama
Houston, TX 77006
713-520-1520
Contact: Richard Tuthill, Music
Editor
Features some reviews

Lubbock

Record Stores

Hasting's Records
4116 19th Street
Lubbock, TX 79401
806-793-1818
Indy Buyer

University Records
711 University Ave.
Lubbock, TX 79401
806-741-0150
Contact: Ken

Radio Stations

KTXT
Texas Technical University
Journalism Building
Lubbock, TX 79408
806-742-3916

San Antonio

Venues

Iries
7920 Fredricksburg Road
San Antonio, TX
512-699-6313
Contact: Charles Esparza
Reggae
Outdoor club

Record Stores

Apple Records
6722 San Pedro
San Antonio, TX 78216
512-824-6588

Hog Wild Records
1824 North Main Street
San Antonio, TX 78212
512-733-5354
Contact: Dave Risher

Sound Warehouse
5545 Northwest Loop 410, Suite 105
San Antonio, TX 78238
512-680-6171, 512-377-2389
Contact: Eric Finley or Karen
Fleig

Radio Stations

KSYM
San Antonio College
1300 San Pedro Ave.
San Antonio, TX 78242
512-733-2800

San Marcos

Venues

Cheatum Street Warehouse
1 Cheatum Street
San Marcos, TX 78666
512-353-9341
Contact: Finlay

Sundance Records
138 North LBJ
San Marcos, TX 78666
512-392-7084
Contact: Greg Ellis

Record Stores

Platters Records
202 B. University Drive
San Marcos, TX 78666
512-353-0888
Indy Buyer

Waco

Record Stores

Sound Warehouse
1118 South Valley Mills
Waco, TX 76711
817-753-7500
Contact: Helene Dube

Radio Stations

KWBU
Baylor University
Castellano Community Building
Waco, TX 76703
817-752-5015

Miscellaneous Texas

Venues

Boulevard
3695 Phelon Blvd., Suite 100
Beaumont, TX 77706
409-832-2753
Contact: Jim Pool
R & B, country and western, and old rock

Morgansterns
4410 College Main
Brian, TX 77801

Endless Horizons
2525 Andrews Hgwy.
Odessa, TX 79762
915-332-7881

Record Stores

Off the Wall Records
1341 Butternut
Abilene, TX 79602
915-676-7424
Indy Buyer

Seldom Scene Records
1933 Belt Line Road
Carrolton, TX 75006
214-418-0270
Indy Buyer

Budget Music & Video
6611 Everhart Ave.
Corpus Christi, TX 78413
512-855-6911
Contact: David Cantu

RPM Records
927 West Centerville
Garland, TX 75041
214-681-8441
Contact: Randall Frierson

MDI Distribution
1174 113th Street
Grand Prairie, TX 75050
214-660-1976
Contact: Roger Christian

Forever Young Records
1221 West Airport Freeway, #205
Irving, TX 75062
214-252-4686
Contact: Phillip Moore

Hasting's Books and Records
3512 Knickerbocker
San Angelo, TX 76904
915-944-7101
Contact: Sandra Medders

Yellow Rose Records
1805 South Lincoln
San Angelo, TX 76904
915-944-7455
Contact: Dan

Radio Stations

KKOM
P.O. Box BB
Et Station,
Commerce, TX 75428
214-886-5848

KLAQ
4141 Pinnacle, Suite 120
El Paso, TX 79902
915-544-8864

KUDF
University of Texas-El Paso
Mass Communications Department
El Paso, TX 79968
915-747-5000

KSHU
Sam Houston University
P.O. Box 2297
Huntsville, TX 77341
713-294-1354, 713-294-1346

KTBC
3007 Martinsville Road
Nacogdoches, TX 75961
409-564-3724

Press

Music News Magazine
P.O. Box 1162
League City, TX 77573
713-778-4119
Contact: Kevin Wildman

UTD Mercury
P.O. Box 830668
Richardson, TX 75083

GREAT LAKES

- [x] Illinois
- [x] Indiana
- [x] Michigan
- [x] Minnesota
- [x] Ohio
- [x] Wisconsin

I L L I N O I S

Carbondale

Venues

Gatsby's
608 West Illinois
Carbondale, IL 62901
618-529-9150
Contact: Robbie Stokes

Hanger Nine
P.O. Box 446
Carbondale, IL 62901
618-549-0511
Contact: Richard Simpson

Record Stores

Plaza Records
825 South Illinois Ave.
Carbondale, IL 62901
618-549-5423
Contact: Kim

Radio Stations

WIDB
Southern Illinois University
Fourth Floor Student Center
Carbondale, IL 62901
618-536-2361

Press

Daily Egyptian
Communications Building
Southern Illinois University
Carbondale, IL 62901
618-536-3311
Contact: Entertainment Editor
University newspaper

Champaign

Venues

Mable's
P.O. Box J Station A
Champaign, IL 61820
217-328-5701
Contact: John Marshall
Large national acts
Devoted weekend following

Trito's
601 East Green Street
Champaign, IL 61820
217-337-5030
Contact: Chris Corpora
College music

Record Stores

Record Service, Inc.
621 East Green Street
Champaign, IL 61820
217-384-7227, 217-344-6222
Contact: Phil Strang

Record Swap
606½ East Green Street
Champaign, IL 61820
217-351-9047
Contact: Bob Diener

Radio Stations

WPGU
204 East Peabody Drive
Champaign, IL 61820
217-333-2016

Charleston

Venues

Joe's Garage
509 Vanberan
Charleston, IL 61920
217-345-2380
Contact: Joe Wiltermod
Original rock 'n' roll

Radio Stations

WEIU
Eastern Illinois University
139 Buzzard
Charleston, IL 61920
217-581-3710

Chicago

The Windy City seemed to have lost its progressive wind for a while; however, all indications show that it is very much on the rise. With some new clubs and great radio stations, the crowds and bands are coming out of the woodwork. There are a plethora of other clubs not listed, but those are mainly blues clubs — Chicago's got the best.

Venues

Cabaret Metro
3730 North Clark
Chicago, IL 60613
312-549-4140
Contact: Joe Shannahan
Mostly rock 'n' roll

Club 950
950 West Wrightwood
Chicago, IL 60614
312-929-8955
Contact: Noa

Cubby Bear
1059 West Addison
Chicago, IL 60613
312-327-1662
Contact: Sue Miller
Mostly rock 'n' roll

Exit, The
1653 North Wells
Chicago, IL 60614
312-440-0535

Medusa's
3257 North Sheffield
Chicago, IL 60657
312-935-3635
Contact: Dave Shelton

Record Stores

Dr. Wax Records
2529 North Clark Street
Chicago, IL 60614
312-549-3377
Contact: Dan Scanlon

Downtown Records
34 East Oak Street
Chicago, IL 60611
312-649-0922
Contact: Kevin Farley

Gramaphone Records
2663 North Clark Street
Chicago, IL 60614
312-472-3683
Contact: Joe Dale

Imports Etc.
711 South Plymouth Court
Chicago, IL 60605
312-922-3143
Contact: Paul Weisberg

Kroozin
4069 South Archer
Chicago, IL 60632
312-254-6264
Contact: Tom Brown

Peaches Records
7601 South Cicero
Chicago, IL 60652
312-735-3957
Contact: Jack Buscio

Record Exchange
1041 West Belmont
Chicago, IL 60657
312-975-9285
Contact: Wilbur

Record Hunt
5951 West Lawrence
Chicago, IL 60630
312-685-7113
Contact: Billy Corgan

Roadmaster Records
1905 West Howard Street
Chicago, IL 60626
312-338-5555
Contact: Garfield

Rock Records
175 West Washington
Chicago, IL 60602
312-346-3489
Contact: Mike or Barb

Rolling Stones Records
7300 West Irving Park Road
Chicago, IL 60634
312-456-0861
Contact: Lee Swanson

Rose Records
3010 North Oakley
Chicago, IL 60618
312-281-8444
Contact: Katherine or Tom Jacobson

Rose Records
214 South Wabash
Chicago, IL 60604
312-987-9044
Contact: Steve Goedde

Round Records
6560 North Sheridan Road
Chicago, IL 60626
312-338-5762
Contact: Steve Krater

Sound Track Records
5552 West North Avenue
Chicago, IL 60639
312-637-0840
Contact: Oshun Gadiye

Wax Trax Records
2449 North Lincoln Ave.
Chicago, IL 60614
312-929-0221, 312-528-8753
Contact: Mark Clifton

Radio Stations

WBEZ
105 West Adams, 40th Floor
Chicago, IL 60603
312-890-8225
Contact: Ken Davis, Program Director

WCRX
Columbia College, Suite 709
600 South Michigan Ave.
Chicago, IL 60605-1996
312-663-1693
Contact: Jim Modelski, Program Director

WDPU
DePaul University
2345 North Clifton Ave.
Chicago, IL 60614
312-341-8404

WGCI
332 South Michigan
Chicago, IL 60604
312-984-1400

WHPK
University of Chicago
5706 South University Ave.
Chicago, IL 60637
312-702-8289

WNIB/WNIZ
1140 West Erie Street
Chicago, IL 60622
312-633-9700
Contact: Ron Ray, Program Director

WXRT
4949 West Belmont Ave.
Chicago, IL 60641
312-777-1700
Contact: Norm Winer, Program
Director

WZRD
Northeastern Illinois University
5500 North St. Louis Ave.
Chicago, IL 60625
312-583-4780, X2861

Press

Chicago Music Magazine
842 West Grace, Third Floor
Chicago, IL 60613
312-525-7553
Contact: Mike Macharello, Editor

Chicago Reader
P.O. Box 11101
Chicago, IL 60611
312-828-0350

Chicago Sun-Times
401 North Wabash
Chicago, IL 60611
312-321-3000
Contact: Robert Marsh, Music Editor

Chicago Tribune
435 North Michigan Ave.
Chicago, IL 60611
312-222-3232
Contact: Richard Christiansen,
Entertainment Editor

Entertainer
P.O. Box 288679
Chicago,IL 60628
312-995-0126
Contact: Guy

Learner Paper
1647 West Belmont
Chicago, IL 60657
312-281-7500
Contact: Kim Okabe, Music Editor

DeKalb

Venues

Jungle, The
1027 West Hillcrest
DeKalb, IL 60115
815-758-6609
Contact: Lido Nepomiachi
New wave, rock 'n' roll, and reggae

Record Stores

Appletree Records
1022 West Lincoln Hgwy.
DeKalb, IL 60115
815-758-6420
Contact: Mark Gribble

Record Revolution
817 West Lincoln Hgwy.
DeKalb, IL 60115
815-756-6242
Contact: Mark Cerny

Radio Stations

WKDI
Northern Illinois University
544 College Ave.
DeKalb, IL 60115
815-753-1278

Press

Big Yeah
P.O. Box 127
DeKalb, IL 60115

Evanston

Record Stores

Vintage Vinyl
925 Davis Street
Evanston, IL 60201
312-328-2899
Contact: Steve

Radio Stations

WNUR
Northwestern University
1905 Sheridan Road
Evanston, IL 60201
312-491-7101

La Grange

Radio Stations

WLTL
Lyons Township High School
100 South Brainard Ave.
La Grange, IL 60525
312-482-9585

Press

Wholesome
630 Spring Ave.
La Grange, IL 60525
312-348-5364
Contact: Dave

Macomb

Venues

Change of Pace
226 North Lafayette
Macomb, IL 61455
309-833-2834
Contact: John Wilber
Rock 'n' roll

Radio Stations

WIUS
Western Illinois University
432 Memorial Hall
Macomb, IL 61455
309-298-3217

Peoria

Venues

Juice Bar, The
1300 Siota
Peoria, IL 61614
309-682-3110
Contact: Dave Childs

Radio Stations

WCBU
1501 West Bradley Ave.
Peoria, IL 61625
309-673-7100

Rock Island

Venues

Rock Island Brewing Company
1815 Second Ave.
Rock Island, Il 61201
309-793-1999
Contact: Jerry Ludin
Blues, R & B, and reggae

Record Stores

Co-op Records
3702 14th Ave.
Rock Island, IL 61201
309-788-8012
Contact: Bill Sharp

Miscellaneous Illinois

Record Stores

Bogart's Records
120 East Lake Street
Addison, IL 60101
312-834-4801
Contact: George Watson

The Flip Side, Inc.
918 West Dundee Road
Arlington Heights, IL 60004
312-398-6140
Contact: Lisa Bingora

Off the Record
316 West Northwest Hgwy.
Barrington, IL 60010
312-381-4424
Contact: Jeff Markarion

Hegewisch Discount Records
522 Torrence Ave.
Calumet City, IL 60409
312-891-3020
Contact: Kenny Zurek

Crow's Nest Records
2108 Plainfield Road
Crest Hill, IL 60435
815-725-9196
Contact: Tom Stockenberg

High Living Records
1726 North Milwaukee
Glenview, IL 60025
312-299-2622
Indy Buyer

Record Swap
18061 Dixie Hgwy.
Homewood, IL 60430
312-798-0222
Contact: John

Dog Ear Records
117 West Rockland
Libertyville, IL 60048
312-362-5666
Contact: Peter Prorok

Big Apple Records
1018 South Elmhurst
Mt. Prospect, IL 60056
312-364-0311
Contact: Mark Davis

Wind Records
5420 West 95th Street
Oak Lawn, IL 60453
312-636-0189
Contact: Doreen Wind

Red Tower Records
54 Orland Square Drive
Orland Park, IL 60462
312-349-9200
Contact: Keg or Kevin Giragosian

229 Club Records
4438 Center Terrace
Rockford, IL 61108
815-229-2582
Contact: Rick

Yorktown Music Shoppe
1211 Golf Road
Rolling Meadows, IL 60008
312-843-3220
Contact: Ron Salpictro

Turntable Records
311 West Golf Road
Golf Point Plaza
Schaumburg, IL 60195
312-519-9090
Contact: Bob Cooke

Record City
3956 West Dumpster
Skokie, IL 60076
312-679-7216
Indy Buyer

Rock 'n' Music & Video
851 West Dundee Road
Wheeling, IL 60090
312-541-1717
Contact: Sandra or Bill

Empire in Wilmette
511 Green Bay Road
Wilmette, IL 60091
312-256-0030
Contact: Rick Reger

Off the Record
1135½ Central Ave.
Wilmette, IL 60091
312-251-6525
Contact: Craig Markarian

Radio Stations

WESN
Illinois Wesleyan University
P.O. Box 2900
Bloomington, IL 61701
309-556-2634

WJMU
Milikin University
1184 West Main Street
Decatur, IL 62522
217-424-6377

WDGC
Downers Grove North High School
4436 Main Street
Downers Grove, IL 60515
312-852-0404
Contact: Bob Dedic

WSIE
Southern Illinois University
Campus Box 1773
Edwardsville, IL 62026
618-692-2228

WHCC
Highland College
Pearl City Road
Freeport, IL 61032
815-235-6121

WVKC
Knox College
Galesburg, IL 61401
309-343-9940

WMXM
Lake Forest College
Lake Forest, IL 60045
312-234-5480

WLNX
Lincoln College
300 Keokuk Street
Lincoln, IL 62656
217-735-3495

WSMI
P.O. Box 10
Litchfield, IL 62056
217-324-5921

WRIK
105 West Fifth
P.O. Box 32
Metropolis, IL 62960
618-524-3698

WVJC
Wabash Valley College
2200 College Drive
Mount Carmel, IL 62863
618-262-8989

WZND
Illinois State University-Normal
103 Media Center
Normal, IL 61761
309-438-5491

WAAS
Amos Alonzo Stagg High School
111th and Roberts Road
Palos Hills, IL 60465
312-974-3300

WRRG
Triton College Radio
2000 Fifth Ave.
River Grove, IL 60171
312-456-5165

WLRA
Lewis University
Route 53
Romeoville, IL 60441
815-838-0700

WMRY
1944 Innerbelt Business Center
Drive, Suite 101
St. Louis, IL 63114
314-426-0101

WARG
7329 West 63rd Street
Summit, IL 60501
312-458-3503, 312-458-9274

WNTH
New Trier High School
385 Winnetka Ave.
Winnetka, IL 60093
312-446-4090

INDIANA

Bloomington

Venues

Bluebird
216 North Walnut
Bloomington, IN 47401
812-336-3984
Contact: David Mowery
Original, rock 'n' roll, and blues

Jakes
419 North Walnut Street
Bloomington, IN 47401
812-332-0402
Contact: Lee Williams
National acts and rock 'n' roll

Second Story
201 College Ave.
Bloomington, IN 47401
812-334-3232
Contact: David
Progressive

Record Stores

Discount Den
520 East Kirkwood
Bloomington, IN 47401
812-339-8831
Contact: Rachel Reimers

Karma Records
116 South Indiana Ave.
Bloomington, IN 47401
812-336-1212
Contact: Bill Zink

Ozarka Records
212 South Indiana Ave.
Bloomington, IN 47401
812-334-0717
Contact: Charles Pierce

Wooden Nickel Records
1797 East Tenth Street
Bloomington, IN 47401
812-332-4919
Contact: Cathy Dyar

Radio Stations

WFIU
Indiana University
Radio/TV Building, Room 146
Bloomington, IN 47405
812-335-1357

WIUS
815 East Eighth Street
Bloomington, IN 47401
812-335-9487, 812-335-6709

Evansville

Record Stores

Cat's Records
925 North Park Drive
Evansville, IN 47714
812-428-2287
Contact: Robyn Zigenfuss

Radio Stations

WUEV
University of Evansville
1800 Lincoln Ave.
Evansville, IN 47722
812-479-2022

Indianapolis

Venues

Patio
6308 North Guilford
Indianapolis, IN 46220
317-253-0799
Contact: Pat Rhoda
Original, reggae, rock 'n' roll, blues, and contemporary

Record Stores

Second Time Around Records
6330 North Ferguson
Indianapolis, IN 46220
317-255-8008
Contact: Todd Kennedy

Radio Stations

WFYI
1401 North Meridian Street
Indianapolis, IN 46202
317-636-2020

WICR
1400 East Hanna Ave.
Indianapolis, IN 46227
317-788-3280

Press

New Times, The
P.O. Box 44089
Indianapolis, IN 46204
317-924-3663
Contact: Rick Powell

Miscellaneous Indiana

Record Stores

Karma Records
Keystone Square Mall
2152 East 116th Street
Carmel, IN 46032
317-844-1035

Hegewisch Discount Records
4000 East Lincoln Hgwy.
Merrillville, IN 46410
219-947-1511
Contact: Jeff Scroggins

Radio Stations

WEAX
Tristate University
Stewart Hall
Angola, IN 46703
219-665-3314

WNDY
Wabash College
301 West Wabash
Crawfordsville, IN 47933
317-364-4240

WVPE
Elkhart Area Career Center
2424 California Road
Elkhart, IN 46514
219-262-5660

WECI
Earlham College
Richmond, IN 47374
317-962-3541

WMHD-FM
Rose-Hulman Institute of Technology
5500 Wabash Ave.
Terre Haute, IN 47803
812-877-2623

WLAY
Purdue University
Tarkington Hall
West Lafayette, IN 47906
317-494-2327

Press

Pope, The
306 Zahm Hall
Notre Dame, IN 46556
Contact: Tim Adams

M I C H I G A N

Ann Arbor

Good stop in Michigan because of the large colleges here. As science major Rob Hainer says, "We go out almost every night to see bands."

Venues

Blind Pig
208 South First Street
Ann Arbor, MI 48103
313-996-8555
Contact: Todd Headrick
Wide variety of music

Rick's
611 Church Street
Ann Arbor, MI 48104
313-996-2747
Contact: Lee Berry
All types of music. On campus, a very "in" place to be
Booked by Prism Productions
313-665-4755

University Club
530 South State Street
Ann Arbor, MI 48109
313-763-2236
Contact: Michael Pipkin
Reggae, new wave, and R & B

Record Stores

Schoolkids
523 East Liberty
Ann Arbor, MI 48104
313-994-8031
Contact: Byron Bull

Radio Stations

WCBN
University of Michigan
520 Student Activities
Ann Arbor, MI 48104
313-763-3501

WIQB
P.O. Box 8605
Ann Arbor, MI 48107
313-662-2881

Detroit

A very happenin' jazz scene, but rock 'n' roll it ain't.

Venues

Alvins
5756 Cass Ave.
Detroit, MI 48202
313-832-0589
Contact: Tim McGuire

Paychecks
2932 Caniff
Detroit, MI 48212
313-872-8934
All kinds of music

Radio Stations

WAYN
Wayne State University
6001 Cass
Detroit, MI 48202
313-577-4200

WDET
6001 Cass
Detroit, MI 48202
313-577-4146

WTWR
University of Detroit
4001 West McNichols
Detroit, MI 48221
313-927-1152

Press

Metro Times
800 David Whitney Building
Detroit, MI 48226
313-961-4060
Contact: Toni Swanger, Managing
Editor

Grand Rapids

Record Stores

JR's Music Shop
Woodland Mall
3159 28th Street Southeast
Grand Rapids, MI 49508
616-942-0513
Contact: Robert Copeland

Vinyl Solutions
2055 28th Street Southeast
Grand Rapids, MI 49508
616-241-4040
Contact: Paul Pastalaniec

Radio Stations

WCAL
Calvin College
Grand Rapids, MI 49506
616-957-7055

Press

Little Friend
42 Dennis Street
Grand Rapids, MI 49506
616-456-9857
Contact: Jim Bleek
Quarterly fanzine

Kalamazoo

Record Stores

Boogie Records
773 West Michigan
Kalamazoo, MI 49007
616-385-4288
Contact: Tom Strebel

WJMD
Kalamazoo College
1200 Academy Street
Kalamazoo, MI 49007
616-383-8425

Radio Stations

WIDR
Western Michigan University
1511 Faunce
Student Services Building
Kalamazoo, MI 49008
616-387-6301

Press

Gazette
401 South Burdick
Kalamazoo, MI 49007
616-345-3511
Contact: Doug Pullen

Lansing

Venues

Rick's American Cafe
224 Abbott
East Lansing, MI 48823
517-351-2285
Contact: Terry Stover
Any kind of music

Radio Stations

WLFT
Michigan State University
310 Auditorium
East Lansing, MI 48824
517-353-4414

Record Stores

Flat, Black and Circular
541 East Grand River
East Lansing, MI 48823
517-351-0838
Contact: Dave Bernath

Mount Pleasant

Venues

Tom Foolery
112 West Michigan
Mount Pleasant, MI 48858
517-772-1132
Contact: Harvey

Radio Stations

WCHP
Central Michigan University
28 Anspach Hall, Room 28
Mount Pleasant, MI 48859
517-774-3923

WMHW
Central Michigan University
180 Moore Hall
Mount Pleasant, MI 48859
517-774-7287

Royal Oak

Record Stores

Off The Record
322 South Main
Royal Oak, MI 48067
313-398-4436
Contact: Lee Rosenbloom

Radio Stations

WDFX
306 South Washington, Suite 500
Royal Oak, MI 48067
313-298-6900

Wyoming

Record Stores

Believe in Music, Inc.
1325 28th Street
Wyoming, MI 49509
616-530-3752
Contact: Jerry

Crazy Larry's Records
3920 Plainfield Northeast
Wyoming, MI 49505
616-364-9616, 616-243-5642
Contact: Larry

Radio Stations

WYCE
2820 Clyde Park Southwest
Wyoming, MI 49509
616-530-7506

Miscellaneous Michigan

Record Stores

Rock Cafe Records
647 Capitol Ave. Southwest
Battle Creek, MI 49015
616-962-6622
Contact: Melissa Packett

Music Magic II
1795 M 139
Binton Harbor, MI 49022
616-925-2222
Contact: Michael Douglas

Sam's Jams Records
279 West Nine Mile Road
Ferndale, MI 48220
313-547-SAMS
Indy Buyer

Record Emporium
122 West Hughitt
Iron Mountain, MI 49801
906-779-1561
Contact: Mike Felton

Rock-A-Rolla Records
200 West Main Street
Owosso, MI 48867
517-723-5145

WBKX
Northern Michigan University
West Hall
Marquette, MI 49855
906-227-2349

WWPZ
P.O. Box 286
Petoskey, MI 49770
616-347-8713

WORW
1799 Kraft Road
Port Huron, MI 48060
313-984-2675

WOUX
Oakland University
69 Oakland Center
Rochester, MI 48309-4401
313-370-4272

WNMC
Northwestern Michigan College
1701 East Front Street
Traverse City, MI 49684
616-922-1090

MINNESOTA

Mankato

Record Stores

MSSA Student Exchange Record Department
Mankato State University
P.O. Box 58
Mankato, MN 56001
507-389-2622
Contact: Brian Renfroe

Radio Stations

KRNR
Mankato State University
P.O. Box 46 (B-2)
Gage Towers
Mankato, MN 56001
507-389-5793

Minneapolis

This flourishing music community has a reputation for great talent, and not just Prince or The Replacements. It's an active community, and the local musicians frequent the clubs looking at out-of-towners.

Venues

400 Club
400 Cedar Ave.
Minneapolis, MN 55454
612-332-2903
Contact: Bill
Not too progressive
Contact: JoAnn Dews

Wind, Waves & Wheels, Inc.
198 Northland Drive
Rockford, MI 49341
616-866-9584
Contact: Todd Andrews

Radio Stations

WGVC
Grand Valley State College
98 Fieldhouse
Allendale, MI 49401
616-895-3128

WRKX
Ferris State College
P.O. Box 225
Patrick Building
Big Rapids, MI 49307
616-592-5913

WGHS
20500 West 13 Mile Road
Birmingham, MI 48010
313-645-0322

WHFR
Henry Ford Community College
5101 Evergreen Road
Dearborn, MI 48128
313-845-9676

WUMD
University of Michigan-Dearborn
4901 Evergreen Road
Dearborn, MI 48128
313-593-5167

WLNZ
13105 Schavey Road, Suite 2
Dewitt, MI 48820
517-669-8361

WORB
Oakland Community College
27055 Orchard Lake Road
Farmington Hills, MI 48018
313-471-7789

WWCK
3217 Lapeer Road
Flint, MI 48503
313-744-1570

WTHS
Hope College
Dewitt Center
Holland, MI 49423
616-394-6452

WMTU
Michigan Technological University
West Wads
Houghton, MI 49931
906-487-2333

WJXQ
2900 Shirley Drive
Jackson, MI 49201
517-788-6360

Cabooz
917 Cedar Ave.
Minneapolis, MN 55404
612-338-6425
Contact: Charlie Campbell

First Ave.
P.O. Box 2126
Minneapolis, MN 55402
612-338-8407
Contact: Steve McClellan

Five Corners
501 Cedar Ave.
Minneapolis, MN 55454
612-338-6424
Contact: Brad Jacobson
R & B

Uptown
3018 Hennepin Ave. South
Minneapolis, MN 55408
612-823-4719
Contact: Maggie McPherson
Mostly original rock
One of the best clientele around

Record Stores

Electric Fetus Records
2010 Fourth Ave. South
Minneapolis, MN 55404
612-870-9300

Garage Door Records
2548 Nicollet Ave.
Minneapolis, MN 55404
612-871-0563
Contact: Jim Peterson

Musicland Group, The
7500 Excelsior Blvd.
Minneapolis, MN 55426
612-932-7700
LP Buyer

Musicland
136 Northtown Drive
Minneapolis, MN 55434
612-786-9090
Contact: Julie Dupre

Northern Lights
700 Hennepin Ave.
Minneapolis, MN 55403
612-332-4025
Contact: Ron Clark

Oar Folkjokeopus Records
2557 Lindale Ave. South
Minneapolis, MN 55405
612-872-7400
Contact: Mark Trehus

Platters Record Store
2922 Lyndale Ave. South
Minneapolis,MN 55408
612-822-2528
Contact: Kevin Cole

Positively 4th Street Records
805 Fourth Street Southeast
Minneapolis, MN 55414
612-331-4439
Contact: John Kulstad

Rocket Records
1608 Harmon Place
Minneapolis, MN 55405
612-874-7927
Contact: Diane Barelli

Radio Stations

KFAI
1518 East Lake Street, Suite 209
Minneapolis, MN 55407
612-721-5011

KTCZ
The Butler Square Building
100 North Sixth Street
Minneapolis, MN 55403
612-339-0000

WMMR
328 Coffman Memorial Union
300 Washington Ave. Southeast
Minneapolis, MN 55455
612-625-5926, 612-625-8942

Press

City Pages
P.O. Box 59183
Minneapolis, MN 55459
612-375-1015
Contact: Michael Welch, Music
Editor

Power for Living
2521 Irving Ave. South
Minneapolis, MN 55405
612-874-0358
Contact: David Roth
Bi-monthly fanzine

Twin City Reader
5500 Wayzata Blvd.
Minneapolis, MN 55416
612-591-2500
Contact: Tom Surowicz, Music
Editor

St. Paul

Record Stores

Northern Lights Records
1451 University Ave.
St. Paul, MN 55104
612-645-8004
Contact: Dee Traxler

Radio Stations

WMCN
Macalester College Radio
1600 Grand Ave.
St. Paul, MN 55105
612-696-6507

Miscellaneous Minnesota

Record Stores

Last Place On Earth Records
33 East Superior Street
Duluth, MN 55802
218-727-1244
Indy Buyer

Radio Stations

KAVT
Austin Technical Institute
1900 Eighth Ave. Northwest
Austin, MN 55912
507-433-0641

KBSB
Bemidji State University
1500 Birtchmont Drive
Bemidji, MN 56601
218-755-2059

KSJU
St. Johns University
Collegeville, MN 56321
612-363-3380

KQRS
917 North Lilac Drive
Golden Valley, MN 55422
612-545-5601

KUMM
University of Minnesota-Morris
Morris, MN 56267
612-589-2211

KRLX
Carleton College
Northfield, MN 55057
507-663-4127

KRPR
Rochester Community College
Highway 14 East
Rochester, MN 55904
507-285-7231

KVSC
St. Cloud State University
Learning Resources Center
St. Cloud, MN 56301
612-255-3066

KQAL
Winona State University
Performing Arts Center
Winona, MN 55987
507-457-5226

O H I O

Akron

Record Stores

Akron Records
28 East Exchange Street
Akron, OH 44308
216-376-6212
Indy Buyer

Quonset Hut
1688 West Market Street
Akron, OH 44313
216-836-0016
Contact: Scott

Record Theatre
1100 East Tallmadge Ave.
Akron, OH 44301
216-633-6988
Indy Buyer

Radio Stations

WAUP-FM
Akron, OH 44325-1004
216-375-7105
Contact: Tom Beck

WONE
1735 South Hawkins
Akron, OH 44320
216-869-9800
Contact: Brian Taylor

Athens
Venues

Union Bar and Grill
18 West Union Street
Athens, OH 45701
614-592-9987
Contact: Dave

Radio Stations

ACRN
Ohio University
9 South College
315 Telecommunications Center
Athens, OH 45701
614-593-4910

WATH-AM/WXTO-FM
300 North Columbus Road
Athens, OH 45701
614-593-6651
Conact: Debbie Shrieves

WLHD
Ohio University
East Green Office
Athens, OH 45701
614-597-9759

WOUB
P.O. Box 824
Athens, OH 45701
614-594-5321

WOUC
9 South College Street
Athens, OH 45701
614-593-4554
Contact: Connie Stevens

WSGR
Ohio University
Southern Green Office
Athens, OH 45701
614-597-7458

Bowling Green
Record Stores

Finder's Records
128 North Main Street
Bowling Green, OH 43402
419-352-7677
Contact: Guy Wilcox

WFAL
Bowling Green State University
31 West Hall
Bowling Green, OH 43403
419-372-2195

Radio Stations

WBGU
Bowling Green State University
120 West Hall
Bowling Green, OH 43403
419-372-2826

Cincinnati

"I wouldn't live anywhere else. We get such a great diversity of music coming through here, everything from bluegrass to punk. I love it."
—George Gatch, local yokel

Venues

Bogart's
2621 Vine Street
Cincinnati, OH 45056
513-281-8401, 513-281-8400
Contact: Dan

Clubhouse, The
Ruth Lyons Lane
Cincinnati, OH 45202
513-421-3766

Hap's Old Irish Pub
3508 Erie Ave.
Cincinnati, OH 45208
513-871-9610
Contact: Mrs. Tepe

Plaza
114 West McMillan
Cincinnati, OH 45219
513-281-0426
Contact: Jeff, or Art Morgan

Record Stores

Culture 7 Records
112 West McMillan
Cincinnati, OH 45219
513-751-7772
Contact: Andy Star

Everybody's Records
6106 Montgomery Road
Cincinnati, OH 45213
513-531-4500
Contact: Nolan Benz

Wizard's Records
2629 Vine Street
Cincinnati, OH 45219
513-961-6196
Contact: John James

Radio Stations

WAIF
2525 Victory Pkwy.
Cincinnati, OH 45206
513-961-8900

WVXU
Xavier University
3800 Victory Pkwy.
Cincinnati, OH 45207
513-731-9898
Contact: Chuck Ingram

Press

Cincinnati Post
125 East Court Street
Cincinnati, OH 45202
513-352-2700
Contact: Wayne Perry

Entertainer Magazine
9420 Town Square Ave.
Cincinnati, OH 45242
513-745-9564

Everybody's News
P.O. Box 15625
Cincinnati, OH 45215
513-961-6397
Contact: Mike Gargano
Weekly paper with listings of performing bands

Cleveland

A strong music community both in terms of fans and musicians. No problem shacking up here, everyone is friendly.

Venues

**Agora Metropolitan Theatre &
Ballroom**
5000 Euclid Ave.
Cleveland, OH 44103
216-431-0110
Contact: Joe Millitello
Mostly rock 'n' roll

Aquilon
1575 Meriwinkle
Cleveland, OH 44113
216-781-1575
Contact: Angela
Dressy, chic

Biggies
1187 Old River Road
Cleveland, OH 44113
216-589-9669
Contact: Carol, or Rich Madison
A lot of straight-ahead rock 'n' roll

Brothers Lounge
11609 Detroit Ave.
Cleveland, OH 44102
216-226-3560
Contact: James Rivers
Blues, jazz, and R & B

Euclid Tavern
11629 Euclid Ave.
Cleveland, OH 44106
216-229-7788
Contact: Bob Jost
Blues and rock 'n' roll

Fulton Avenue Cafe
1835 Fulton
Cleveland, OH 44113
216-522-1835
Contact: Gary Sikorski
Jazz and blues

Mardis Gras Lounge and Grill
1423 East 21st Street
Cleveland, OH 44114
216-566-9094
Contact: Nick
Jazz

Pats in the Flats
2233 West Third
Cleveland, OH 44113
216-621-8044
Contact: John Walsh
Everything but disco and classical

Peabody's Down Under
1059 Old River Road
Cleveland, OH 44113
216-241-2451
Contact: Tony Ciulla
Everything but country

Record Stores

Record Den
1774 East 40th
Cleveland, OH 44103
216-391-6464
Contact: Terry Cooper

Shattered Records
12410 Lorain Ave.
Cleveland, OH 44111
216-941-5813
Contact: Frank Conge

Radio Stations

WCPN
3100 Chester Ave., Suite 300
Cleveland, OH 44114-4617
216-432-3700
Contact: Kathleen Cerveny

WCSB
C/O Cleveland State University
956 Rhodes Tower
Cleveland, OH 44115
216-687-3721
Contact: Berni

WRUW
11220 Bellflower Road
Cleveland, OH 44106
216-368-2208
Contact: Melissa Pollack

Press

Plain Dealer
1801 Superior Ave.
Cleveland, OH 44114
216-344-4500
Friday magazine

Scene Magazine
1375 Euclid Ave., Suite 312
Cleveland, OH 44115
Contact: Tracy Benson or Mark Holan

Spotlight Entertainment Magazine
1220 West Sixth, Suite 701
Cleveland, OH 44113
216-241-1760

Cleveland Heights

Venues

Peabody's Cafe
2140 South Taylor Road
Cleveland Heights, OH 44118
216-321-4072
Contact: Dewey Forward
New Wave, rock 'n' roll, and other

Turkey Ridge
1852 Coventry
Cleveland Heights, OH 44118
216-321-7070
Contact: Mark Bock
Blues, country and western, jazz, and top 40

Record Stores

Record Exchange
1780 Coventry Road
Cleveland Heights, OH 44118
216-321-1887
Contact: Marina

Record Revolution
1828 Coventry Road
Cleveland Heights, OH 44118
216-321-7661
Contact: Bob

Wax Stacks Record, Tape & CD Exchange
2254 Lee Road
Cleveland Heights, OH 44118
216-321-7935
Contact: Scott Pickering

Columbus

Venues

Starches
2404 North High Street
Columbus, OH 43202
614-237-4599
Contact: Pete Herman

Record Stores

Buzz Enterprises
333 Highfield Drive
Columbus, OH 43214
614-888-6698
Indy Buyer

Magnolia Thunderpussy Records
1585 North High Street
Columbus, OH 43201
614-421-1511
Contact: Chuck

NY Spotlight and Sounds
201 North 4th Street
Columbus, OH 43215
Contact: Frankie

Radio Stations

WLVQ
42 East Gay Street
Columbus, OH 43215
614-224-1271

WOSR
Ohio State University
Drake Union, Suite 2052
1849 Cannon Drive
Columbus, OH 43210
614-292-9656

Press

Columbus Dispatch
34 South Third Street
Columbus, OH 43216
614-461-5000
Does some reviews

Dayton

Venues

Canal St. Tavern
308 East First Street
Dayton, OH 45402
513-461-9343
Contact: Mick Montgomery
All kinds of music

Gilly's
P.O. Box 166 Wright
Dayton, OH 45409
513-228-8414
Contact: Jenny

Record Stores

Renaissance Music
1924 South Smithville Road
Dayton, OH 45420
513-258-1038

Radio Stations

WDCR
University of Dayton
P.O. Box 104
300 College Park
Dayton, OH 45469
513-229-2664

WDPS
Dayton Career Academy
441 River Corridor Drive
Dayton, OH 45402
513-223-0906

WVUD
University of Dayton
300 College Park Ave.
Dayton, OH 45469
513-229-2041
Contact: Reed Kittridge

WWSU
Wright State University
3640 Colonel Glen Hgwy.
Dayton, OH 45235
513-873-2000
Contact: LouAnn Shockley or John Nelson

Kent
Venues

J.B.'s Lounge
244 North Water Street
Kent, OH 44240
216-678-2774
Contact: George
Rock 'n' roll and progressive

Mother's
135 Franklin Ave.
Kent, OH 44240
216-673-2233
Contact: Tom Creech
Top 40

Record Stores

Heartbeat Records
426 East Main Street
Kent, OH 44240
216-678-6371
Indy Buyer

Spinmore Records
P.O. Box 3172
Kent, OH 44240
216-678-3495
Indy Buyer

Radio Stations

WKSR
Kent State University
Music and Speech Building
Kent, OH 44242
216-672-2131

WKSU-FM
Kent State University
Kent, OH 44242
216-672-3114
Contact: Kate Phillips

Lakewood
Venues

Around the Corner
18616 Detroit Ave.
Lakewood, OH 44107
216-521-4413
Contact: Mickey Krivosh
Blues, rock 'n' roll, singles, duos, and trios

Phantasy Night Club
11802 Detroit Ave.
Lakewood, OH 44107
216-228-6300
Contact: Michelle
Rock 'n' roll, punk, and modern music

Record Stores

Chris' Warped Records
13383 Madison Ave.
Lakewood, OH 44107
216-521-4981
Contact: Chris Andrews

Music and More
15100 Detroit Ave.
Lakewood, OH 44107
216-521-1377
Contact: Gary Fugo

Toledo

Record Stores

Boogie Records
3301 West Central
Toledo, OH 43606
419-536-5683
Indy Buyer

Radio Stations

WXUT
University of Toledo
2801 West Bancroft
Toledo, OH 43606
419-537-4172
Contact: David Rose

Yellow Springs

Venues

Antioch College
795 Livermore Street
Community Government
Yellow Springs, OH 45387
513-767-7331
Wonderful place to play

Radio Stations

WYSO-FM
Antioch College
795 Livermore Street
Community Government
Yellow Springs, OH 45387
513-767-1722
Contact: Brian Gibbons

Miscellaneous Ohio

Venues

Vibrations
12861 Albion Road
North Royalton, OH 44133
216-582-1661
Contact: John Tascar
Classic rock, some country rock, open to other types

Barney Googles Holiday Inn Lounge
4742 Brecksville Road
Richfield, OH 44286
216-659-6151
Contact: Bob Carmack

Tommy's
19015 Old Lake Road
Rocky River, OH 44116
216-331-8686
Contact: Tommy Valore
Oldies, top 40, rock 'n' roll

Record Stores

Record Shoppe
138 Front Street
Berea, OH 44017
216-234-7998
Contact: Dennis Selby

Quonset Hut Records
3235 Cleveland Ave. Northwest
Canton, OH 44709
216-492-1293
Contact: Dana Pinney

Platter Puss Records
679 East 185th Street
Euclid, OH 44119
216-531-6743
Contact: Bruce Parker

Record Exchange
5322 Warrensville Center Road
Maple Heights, OH 44137
216-662-7675
Contact: Jeff Brodsky

Record Exchange Warehouse
761-H Beta Drive
Mayfield Village, OH 44143
216-449-4430
Contact: John, or Richard Shahinian

Camelot Music
1000 Freedom Avenue
North Canton, OH 44720
216-494-2282
Indy Buyer

Record Den
4908 Great Northern Mall
North Olmstead, OH 44070
216-779-4428
Contact: Mike Wieland

Rockpile Records
7425 York Road
Parma, OH 44130
216-884-7755
Contact: Bill Wilkens

Record Exchange
6370 York Road
Parma Heights, OH 44130
216-845-0828

Underdog Records
5429 South Ave.
Youngstown, OH 44512
216-788-3743
Contact: Ron

Radio Stations

WBWC
Baldwin-Wallace College
Berea, OH 44017
216-826-2187
Contact: Promotions

WKHR
17425 Snyder Road
Chagrin Falls, OH 44022
216-543-9646

WSLN
Ohio Wesleyan University
Slocum Hall
Delaware, OH 43015
614-369-4431, X559

WKCO
Kenyon College
Gambier, OH 43022
614-427-3711

WOBC
Oberlin College
Wilder Hall
Oberlin, OH 44074
216-775-8107

WOXY
5120 College Corner Pike
Oxford, OH 45056
513-523-4114
Contact: Kerry, Program Director

WYCC
Miami University
Presser Hall
Oxford, OH 45056
513-529-1269

WUSO
Wittenberg University
P.O. Box 720
Springfield, OH 45501
513-327-7026

WUJC
John Carroll University
20700 North Park Blvd.
University Heights, OH 44118
216-397-4437

Press

Alternative Press
P.O. Box 1141
Aurora, OH 44202
216-562-8688
Contact: Mike Shea
Bi-monthly fanzine

Musician
P.O. Box 1923
Marion, OH 43305

W I S C O N S I N

Appleton

Record Stores

Beggar's Tune Records
17 East College
Appleton, WI 54911
414-231-5353
Contact: Gabe Egeland

Radio Stations

WLFM
Lawrence University
115 South Lawe Street
Appleton, WI 54911
414-735-6566

Kenosha

"Some people say the bratwurst is great here. Well, I like the music."
—Jeff Mendeloff, resident

Venues

Bratt Shop
12304 75th Street
Kenosha, WI 53142
414-857-2011
Contact: Bob Latessa

Radio Stations

KBLE
3520 30th Ave.
Kenosha, WI 53142
414-656-7201

Madison

A great college town with an active music community.

Venues

Club De Wash
636 West Washington
Madison, WI 53703
608-256-3302
Contact: Tony Kellsvig

Headliners
626 University Ave.
Madison, WI 53715
608-257-0666
Contact: Shane Todd
Large bar catering to national acts

Nar Bar
307 West Johnson Street
Madison, WI 53704
608-255-5563
Contact: Tim Nar

O Cayz Corral
Madison, WI 53703
608-256-1348
Contact: Tom or Kay
A bit small but by far the city's grooviest spot

Wisconsin Memorial Union
Room 507 Memorial Union
800 Langdon
Madison, WI 53706
608-262-7754
Contact: Ralph Russo or Esther Rose
On campus, complete with built-in crowd

Record Stores

B-side Records
436 State Street
Madison, WI 53703
608-255-1977
Contact: Ralph Cross
or Steve Manley

Discount Den
555 State Street
Madison, WI 53703
608-251-3331
Contact: Tony Kunz

Discount Records
658 State Street
Madison, WI 53703
608-257-4584
Contact: Rick Halbach

Mad City Music Exchange
1437 Regent Street
Madison, WI 53711
608-251-8558
Contact: Dave Benton

Record Town
138 East Towne Mall
Madison, WI 53704
608-249-5770
Contact: Steve Daubenmier

Wazoo Records
551 State Street
Madison, WI 53703
608-257-7781

Radio Stations

WLHA
University of Wisconsin
Holt Commons
1950 Willow Drive
Madison, WI 53706
608-262-1206

WMAD
P.O. Box 7727
Madison, WI 53707
608-249-9277

WORT
118 South Bedford Street
Madison, WI 53703
608-256-2695

WZEE
Z-104
P.O. Box 8030
Madison, WI 53708
608-274-1070, 608-274-2720

Press

Capital Times
P.O. Box 8060
Madison, WI 53708
608-252-6400
Contact: City Desk

Isthmus
14 West Mifflin Street
Madison, WI 53703
608-251-5627
Contact: Dean Robbins
Weekly paper with listings, some reviews

Thang Magazine
105 South Mills
Madison, WI 53715

Wisconsin State Journal
P.O. Box 8058
Madison, WI 53708
608-252-6100
Contact: Michael St. John

Milwaukee

Recently has become a breeding ground for roots rock (e.g., E.I.E.I.O, The Bodeans, Semi Twang).

Venues

Sweetwater
1127 North Water Street
Milwaukee, WI 53202
414-278-8847
Contact: Carolyn Rebholz

Radio Doctors
240 West Wells
Milwaukee, WI 53203
414-276-6422
Contact: Tim Martin

Record Stores

Atomic Records
1813 East Locust Street
Milwaukee, WI 53211
414-332-3663
Contact: Rich Menning

Auddies One Stop
2204 West North Ave.
Milwaukee, WI 53205
414-342-4636
Contact: Audie

East Side Records
2410 North Murry Ave.
Milwaukee, WI 53211
414-964-5992
Contact: Steve Rogers

Flipside Records
3712 West North Ave.
Milwaukee, WI 53208
414-871-1344
Contact: Hazel Westmoreland

Hot Wax Records
3501 West Capital Drive
Milwaukee, WI 53216
414-444-6864
Indy Buyer

Mainstream Records
3333 South 27th Street
Milwaukee, WI 53215
414-643-6636

Radio Stations

WLZR
5407 West McKinley
Milwaukee, WI 53208
414-453-4130

WMSE
Milwaukee School of Engineering
P.O. Box 644
Milwaukee, WI 53201-0644
414-277-7247

WMUR
Marquette University
1131 West Wisconsin Ave.
Milwaukee, WI 53233
414-224-3393

Press

Milwaukee Journal
P.O. Box 661
Milwaukee, WI 53201
414-224-2000
Contact: Tom Strini, Music Editor

Milwaukee Sentinel
P.O. Box 371
Milwaukee, WI 53201
414-224-2000
Contact: Nancy Miller, Music Editor

Oshkosh
Venues

B & B
686 North Main
Oshkosh, WI 54901
414-235-6421
Contact: Wally Wagner

Eagles Club
405 Washington Ave.
Oshkosh, WI 54901
414-231-6040
Contact: John Stenz, Jr.

Reeve Memorial Union
748 Algoma Blvd.
Oshkosh, WI 54901
414-424-2345
Contact: Rich Naumann

Radio Stations

WRST
University of Wisconsin
800 Algoma Blvd.
Oshkosh, WI 54901
414-424-3113

Miscellaneous Wisconsin
Record Stores

Mainstream Records
4820 South 76th Street
Greenfield, WI 53220
414-282-7780
Contact: Gary Edwards

Radio Stations

WBCR
Beloit College
P.O. Box 39
700 College Street
Beloit, WI 53511
608-365-3391, X402

WBSD
225 Robert Street
Burlington, WI 53105
414-763-6532

WUEC
University of Wisconsin-Eau Claire
170 Fine Arts Center
Eau Claire, WI 54701
715-836-4170

WGBW
University of Wisconsin
2420 Nicolet Drive
Green Bay, WI 54311-7001
414-465-2448
Contact: Kris Wenze, Music Director

WVSS
Stout University
120 Broadway
Menominee, WI 54754
715-232-2332

WSUP
One University Plaza
42 Pioneer Tower
Platteville, WI 53818
608-342-1165

WWSP
University of Wisconsin
101 Communication Arts Center
Stevens Point, WI 54481
715-346-2696

KUWS
University of Wisconsin-Superior
1800 Grand Ave.
Superior, WI 54880
715-394-8404

WCCX
Carrol College
221 North East Ave.
Waukesha, WI 53186
414-524-7355

WYRE
University of Wisconsin-Waukesha
1500 University Drive
Waukesha, WI 53188
414-521-5201

Press

Goldmine
700 East State Street
Iola, WI 54990
715-445-2214
Contact: Jeff Tamarkin

DEEP SOUTH

- Alabama
- Arkansas
- Florida
- Georgia
- Kentucky
- Louisiana
- Tennessee

A L A B A M A

Birmingham

Venues

Nick, The
2514 Tenth Ave. South
Birmingham, AL 35205
205-252-3831
Contact: Dan Nolan
Basic alternative club — plays all styles of music

Record Stores

Charlemagne Records
1924½ 11th Ave. South
Birmingham, AL 35205
205-322-5349
Contact: Marian McKay

Wuxtry Records
3156 Cahaba Heights Village
Birmingham, AL 35243
205-967-7866
Contact: Chuck Connolly

Radio Stations

WBHM
1028 Seventh Ave. South
Birmingham, AL 35294
205-934-2606

Tuscaloosa

Venues

Ivory Tusk
1215 University Blvd.
Tuscaloosa, AL 35401
205-752-3435
Contact: Bill Newton
University-oriented music

Record Stores

Vinyl Solution
1207 University Blvd.
Tuscaloosa, AL 35401
205-758-3710
Contact: George Hadjidakis or Mark Patrick

Radio Stations

WUAL
University of Alabama
P.O. Box 870370
Tuscaloosa, AL 35487-0370
205-348-6644

WVUA
University of Alabama
P.O. Box D
Tuscaloosa, AL 35487
205-348-6082

Press

Crimson White
P.O. Drawer A
University of Alabama
Tuscaloosa, AL 35487
205-348-6144
Contact: Amanda Crowell
Thursday music section

Miscellaneous Alabama
Radio Stations

WEGL-FM
Auburn University
1239 Haley Center
Auburn, AL 36849
205-826-4057, 205-826-1648

WEXP
Gadsen Street Junior College
100 Wallance Drive
Gadsen, AL 35999
205-546-0484

WZEW
118 North Royal, Suite 711
Mobile, AL 36602
205-432-0102

A R K A N S A S

Conway
Record Stores

Doctor Gonzo Records
925 Oak
Conway, AR 72032
501-329-3052
Indy Buyer

KUCA
University of Central Arkansas
P.O. Box 4911
Conway, AR 72032
501-450-3161

Radio Stations

KHDX
Hendrix College
Conway, AR 72032
501-450-1312

Fayetteville
Venues

George's Majestic Lounge
519 West Dickson
Fayetteville, AR 72701
501-442-9788
Contact: Burett Waggoner
Open air

Lilly's
404 West Dickson
Fayetteville, AR 72701
501-442-9776
Contact: Mack or Joe
Rock 'n' roll

Record Stores

Record Exchange
632 West Dickson
Fayetteville, AR 72701
501-443-2345
Contact: Glen Wheeler

Radio Stations

KKEG
1780 Holly Street
P.O. Box 878
Fayetteville, AR 72702
501-521-5566

KRFA
University of Arkansas
Fayetteville, AR 72701
501-575-2557

Little Rock

Venues

S.O.B., The
1321 East Second Street
Little Rock, AR 72202
501-372-5570
Plays everything

White Water Tavern
2500 West Seventh Street
Little Rock, AR 72205
501-374-3801
Contact: Larry Garrison
R & B and blues

Record Stores

Arkansas Record & CD Exchange
4212 MacArthur
Little Rock, AR 72118
501-753-7877
Contact: Bill Eginton

Been Around Records
1720 South University
Little Rock, AR 72204
501-663-8767
Contact: John Harris

Discount Records
3400 South University
Little Rock, AR 72204
501-565-9848
Contact: Lance or Steve Harrison

Peaches
4808 JFK Blvd.
Little Rock, AR 72116
501-771-0055
Contact: Eddie Tilley

Radio Stations

KABF
1501 Arch
Little Rock, AR 72202
501-372-6119

KLRE-KUAR
2801 South University, Seventh Floor
Little Rock, AR 72204
501-569-8485

KUAR
2801 South University, Seventh Floor
Little Rock, AR 72204
501-562-5573

Press

Arkansas Gazette
112 West Third
Little Rock, AR 72201
501-371-3700
Contact: Mark Marymont
Strong coverage

Spectrum
1300 South Main Street, Suite B
Little Rock, AR 72202
501-375-7732
Contact: Steven Buel

Miscellaneous Arkansas
Venues

Center Street Cafe
10 Center Street
Eureka Springs, AR 72632
501-253-8102
Contact: Manny

Record Stores

Joker Records
114 North Commerce
Russellville, AR 72801
501-967-5181
Contact: Alan Souheaver

F L O R I D A

Fort Lauderdale
Venues

Confetti's Reunion Room
2660 East Connecticut Blvd.
Fort Lauderdale, FL
305-776-4080

Press

Twist Magazine
P.O. Box 292336
Fort Lauderdale, FL 33309
305-963-1286
Contact: Joel Fader, Editor

Gainesville
Record Stores

Hyde and Zeke Records
1620 West University Ave.
Gainesville, FL 32603
904-376-1687
Contact: Bill Perry or Charlie Scales

WUFT-FM
University of Florida
2104 Weimer Hall
Gainesville, FL 32611
904-392-5200

Radio Stations

WRUF
University of Florida
P.O. Box 14444
Gainesville, FL 32604
904-392-0771

Press

Jazziz
P.O. Box 8309
Gainesville, FL 32605-8309
904-375-3705
Contact: Michael Fagien

Melbourne
Record Stores

Record Bar
1701 West New Haven Ave.
Melbourne, FL 32901
407-724-6040
Contact: Eddie Presley

Radio Stations

WFIT
Florida Institute of Technology
150 West University Blvd.
Melbourne, FL 32901
407-729-9348

Miami

Venues

Cameo Theatre
1445 Washington
Miami, FL 33139
305-532-0922
Contact: Paco

Club Nu
245 22nd Street
Miami Beach, FL 33139
305-672-0068
Contact: Norman Bedford
New Wave to big band

Fire & Ice
3841 Northeast Second Ave.
Miami, FL 33137
305-573-3473
Contact: Adam Averancon
New Wave

Record Stores

Cocoanuts
14700 Biscayne Blvd.
Miami, FL 33184
305-944-6952
Contact: Wes McCraven

Open Books and Records
44 Northwest 167th Street
Miami, FL 33169
305-940-8750
Contact: Leslie Wimmer

Spec's Music
1666 Northwest 82nd Ave.
Miami, FL 33126
305-592-7288
Contact: Sandy Griffith

Yesterday and Today Records
6800 Southwest 40th
Miami, FL 33155
305-665-3305
Contact: Jon Tovar

Radio Stations

WDNA
P.O. Box 558636
Miami, FL 33155
305-264-9362

WLRN
Public Radio for Florida
172 Northeast 15th Street
Miami, FL 33132
305-376-1717

WIMI
3225 Aviation Ave.
Miami, FL 33133
305-856-9393

Orlando

Record Stores

Murmur Records
709 West Smith Street
Orlando, FL 32804
407-841-3050
Contact: Eddy Foeller

Radio Stations

WUCF
University of Central Florida
4000 Central Florida Blvd.
Orlando, FL 32816
407-275-2133

Tampa/St. Petersburg

The pay is OK, but appreciation for music is limited.

Venues

Act 4
1204 Franklin Street
Tampa, FL 33607
813-229-9098, 813-221-1791
Contact: Scooter

Upstairs At El Gordos
7815 Blind Pass Road
St. Petersburg, FL 33706
813-360-5947
Contact: Bill Wilkins
Reggae and rock 'n' roll

Record Stores

Alternative Records, The
11900 North Nebraska Ave., Suite 3
Tampa, FL 33612
813-977-6383
Contact: Pete Barlas

Vinyl Fever
1502 East Fletcher Ave.
Tampa, FL 33612
813-972-1331
Contact: Dan Diner

Radio Stations

WMNF
1210 East Bufflo Ave.
Tampa, FL 33603
813-238-8001

WUSF
University of South Florida
4202 East Fowler Ave.
Tampa, FL 33620
813-974-4890

Miscellaneous Florida

Venues

Beach Pub
5501 Shore Blvd.
Gulfport, FL 33707
813-347-2005
Contact: Joe Withrow
Many styles of music

Button South
100 Ansin Blvd.
Hallandale, FL 33009
305-454-0001

Respectable Street Cafe
518 Clematis Street
West Palm Beach, FL 33401
407-832-9999
Contact: Rodney Mayo
Progressive and reggae

Swamp Club
5413 Shore Blvd. South
Gulfport, FL 33707
813-327-4505
Contact: Ken
Light rock 'n' roll and pop

Record Stores

Peaches Entertainment
9880 Northwest 77th Ave.
Hialeah Gardens, FL 33016
305-558-0323
Contact: Gail Fokolow

Radio Stations

WVUM-FM
University of Miami
Stanford Drive
P.O. Box 248191
Coral Gables, FL 33124
305-284-3131

WRXK
P.O. Box 9600
Estero, FL 33928
813-332-3696

WSFP-FM
811 College Pkwy.
Areca Hall #216
Ft. Myers, FL 33919
813-489-9580

WFIN
Jacksonville University
2800 University Blvd. North
Jacksonville, FL 32211
904-744-3950

WJCT
100 Festival Park Ave.
Jacksonville, FL 32202
904-358-6349

WKGC
Gulf Coast Community College
5230 West Highway 98
Panama City, FL 32401
904-769-5241

WUWF
University of West Florida
1100 University Pkwy.
Pensacola, FL 32514
904-474-2327

WSRZ
1751 City Island Road
Sarasota, FL 34236
813-388-3936

WKPX
8000 Northwest 44th Street
Sunrise, FL 33351
305-572-1321

WFSU
2561 Pottsdamer
Tallahassee, FL 32304
904-487-3305

WPRK Radio
Rollins College
P.O. Box 2745
Winter Park, FL 32789
407-646-2398

G E O R G I A

Athens

Venues

40 Watt Club
256 West Clayton
Athens, GA 30601
404-549-7871
Contact: Jared Bailey

Fabulous Rockfish Palace, The
433 East Hancock
Athens, GA 30606
404-549-0624
Contact: J. R. Green

Uptown Lounge
140 East Washington Street
Athens, GA 30601
404-353-3405
Contact: Kyle Pilgrim

Record Stores

Ruthless Records
114 College Ave.
Athens, GA 30601
404-548-9099
Contact: Davey Giles

Wuxtry Records
201 College Ave.
Athens, GA 30601
404-353-9303
Contact: Dana Downs

Radio Stations

WUOG
P.O. Box 2065
University of Georgia
Tate Student Center
Athens, GA 30602
404-542-8466

Press

Athens Observer
P.O. Box 112
Athens, GA 30603
404-548-9300
Contact: Betsy Shearron

Red & Black
123 North Jackson Street
Athens, GA 30601
404-543-1791
Contact: Carla May

Atlanta

Venues

Club Rio
195 Luckie Street
Atlanta, GA 30303
404-525-7467
Contact: Michele Rhea or Clay
Jennings
Variety of progressive rock

Metroplex
388 Marietta Northwest
Atlanta, GA 30313
404-523-2631, 404-525-9193
Contact: Paul Cornwell
Rock 'n' roll, reggae and heavy metal

White Dot, The
279 Ponce de Leone
Atlanta, GA 30308
404-872-4833
Contact: Pam or Steve

Record Stores

Wax N Fax Records
432 Moreland Ave. Northeast
Atlanta, GA 30307
404-525-2275
Contact: Danny Beard

Radio Stations

WABE
740 Bismarck Road Northeast
Atlanta, GA 30324
404-827-8900

WRAS
Georgia State University
University Plaza
Atlanta, GA 30303
404-651-2240

WREK
Georgia Tech
Atlanta, GA 30332
404-894-2468

WRFG
P.O. Box 5332
Atlanta, GA 30307
404-523-3471

Press

Atlanta Journal
72 Marietta Street Northwest
Atlanta, GA 30303
404-526-5151
Contact: Russ Devault

Creative Loafing
750 Willoughby
Atlanta, GA 30312
404-688-5623
Contact: Tony Paris or David T. Lindsay
Free Wednesday weekly with weekend listings

Augusta

Venues

Red Line
1936 Walton Way
Augusta, GA 30904
404-733-6400
Contact: Jenny Berlin
Ridiculous booking policies
Not open to independents

Record Stores

Home Folks News and Records
Southgate Plaza
Augusta, GA 30906
404-793-9153
Contact: Margaret Kitchens

Miscellaneous Georgia

Record Stores

Rock 'N' Easy Records
4420 Altama Ave.
Brunswick, GA 31520
912-264-8288
Contact: Dick Gardner

Wuxtry Records
2096 North Decatur Road
Decatur, GA 30033
404-329-0020
Contact: Mark Methe or Chris Mills

Starship Records
6753 Jonesmill Court
Norcross, GA 30092
404-448-9520
Indy Buyer

Turtle's Records
5480 Peachtree, Industrial Blvd.

KENTUCKY

Lexington

Record Stores

Cut Corner Records
377 South Limestone
Lexington, KY 40508
606-273-2673
Contact: Gordon Brown

Radio Stations

WRFL
University of Kentucky
P.O. Box 777
University Station
Lexington, KY 40506
606-257-4082

Uptown Records
210 East Main
Lexington, KY 40507
606-252-4828
Contact: Tony

Louisville

Venues

Tewligan's Tavern
1047 Bandstown Road
Louisville, KY 40204
502-458-2013

Ear X-tacy Records
2431 Baardstown Road
Louisville, KY 40205
502-452-1799
Contact: John Timmons

Radio Stations

WLCV
Suite 41, Student Center
University of Louisville
Louisville, KY 40292
502-588-6966

WPFK
Louisville Free Public Library
301 York Street
Louisville, KY 40203
502-561-8640

Record Stores

Better Days Records
2710 Frankfurt Ave.
Louisville, KY 40206
502-893-3472
Contact: Ben Jones

WUOL
University of Louisville
Louisville, KY 40292
502-588-6467

Press

Courier Journal
525 West Broadway
Louisville, KY 40202
502-582-4011
Contact: Ronni Lundy

Owensboro

Record Stores

Disc Jockey Records
Town Square Mall
Owensboro, KY 42301
502-683-0167
Contact: Lorna Bryant

Radio Stations

WKWC
P.O. Box 1039
3000 Frederics Street
Owensboro, KY 42302-1039
502-685-5937
Shamblee, GA 30341
404-455-6133
Contact: Clint Ard

Radio Stations

WWGC
West Georgia College
Carrollton, GA 30118
404-836-6459

WGHR
Southern College of Technology
1112 Clay Street
Marietta, GA 30060
404-424-7300

WXGC
Georgia College
Mayfair H1
P.O. Box 3124
Milledgeville, GA 31061
912-453-4101

WXVH
409 East Liberty Street
Savannah, GA 31401
912-238-0911

WVGS
Georgia Southern College
P.O. Box 11619, Landrum
Statesboro, GA 30460
912-681-5525

WVVS
Valdosta State College
P.O. Box 142
Valdosta, GA 31698
912-333-5660

Miscellaneous Kentucky

Radio Stations

WMBS
P.O. Box 1340
Murray, KY 42071
502-759-1300

LOUISIANA

Baton Rouge

Venues

Chimes
3357 Highland Road
Baton Rouge, LA 70802
504-383-1754
Contact: Tim Hood
R & B and rock 'n' roll

Record Stores

New Generation Records
10100 Florida Blvd.
Baton Rouge, LA 70815
504-272-1700
Contact: Selisa Hue

Radio Stations

WBRH
2825 Government Street
Baton Rouge, LA 70806
504-383-3243

KLSU
Louisiana State University
B46 Hodges Hall
103 East Stadium
Baton Rouge, LA 70803
504-388-5911

Press

Gris Gris
2431 South Arcadian Throughway
#590
Baton Rouge, LA 70808
504-927-5437
Contact: Johnny Palazzotto

Hammond

Venues

Brady's
110 South West Railroad Ave.
Hammond, LA 70401
504-542-6333
Contact: David Palmer
Reggae, blues, and jazz

Radio Stations

WHMD
P.O. Box 1829
Hammond, LA 70404
504-345-1070

Lafayette

Venues

Grant Street Dance Hall
113 West Grant Street
Lafayette, LA 70501
318-237-8513
Contact: George Baumgartner

Record Stores

Racoon Records
2928 Johnston
Lafayette, LA 70503
318-234-5972
Contact: Lem Sylvest

Radio Stations

KRVS
P.O. Box 42171
Lafayette, LA 70504
318-231-5668

New Orleans

Of course, some great jazz has been and still is being produced here. However, the underground rock scene has something to offer as well. The university crowd really enjoys life and will supply fun and rowdiness.

Venues

Jimmy's Club
8200 Willow Street
New Orleans, LA 70118
504-861-8200
Contact: Jim
More metal and new wave

Maple Leaf
8316 Oak Street
New Orleans, LA 70118
504-866-9359
Contact: John Parson

Tipitina's
501 Napolean Blvd.
New Orleans, LA 70115
504-891-8477
Contact: Sonny Schneidau
Rock 'n' roll, R & B, and funk

Record Stores

Mushroom Records
1037 Broadway
New Orleans, LA 70118
504-866-6065
Contact: Dave

Record Ron's
1129 Decatur Street
New Orleans, LA 70116
504-524-9444
Contact: Ron

Rock N Roll Records and Collectibles
1214 Decatur Street
New Orleans, LA 70116
504-561-5683

Sound Warehouse
5500 Magazine Street
New Orleans, LA 70115
504-891-4026
Contact: Roger Burgett

Radio Stations

WTUL
Tulane University Center
New Orleans, LA 70118
504-865-5887

WWNO
University of New Orleans
Lakefront Campus
New Orleans, LA 70148
504-286-7000

Press

Wavelength Magazine
P.O. Box 15667
New Orleans, LA 70175
504-895-2342
Very good, local supportive paper

Shreveport

Venues

Humphrees
P.O. Box 176
Shreveport, LA 71106
318-227-0845
Contact: Bill Griffin

Record Stores

Sooto Records
205 East Kings Hgwy.
Shreveport, LA 71104
318-865-5681
Contact: Adam Giblin

Stan's Record Shop
7720 Linwood Ave., Suite E
Shreveport, LA 71106
318-687-3661
Contact: Lenny Lewis

Radio Stations

KSCL
Centenary College
2911 Centenary Blvd.
Shreveport, LA 71104
318-869-5297

Miscellaneous Louisiana

Record Stores

The Music Centers
1446 North Airline Hgwy.
Gonzales, LA 70737
504-644-3062
Contact: Wayne Davis

Gold Mine Records
6469 Jefferson Hgwy.
Harahan, LA 70123
504-737-2233
Contact: Rodger Castillo

Odyssey Records
3920 Dublin Street
Nola, LA 70118
504-486-8108
Contact: Gary Holzenthal

Radio Stations

KNLU
128 Stubbs Hall
Monroe, LA 71209
318-342-4073

KNWD
Northwestern State University
P.O. Box 3038
Natchitoches, LA 71457
318-357-5693

KLPI
Radio Tech
P.O. Box 8638
Tech Station
Ruston, LA 71272
318-257-3689

MISSISSIPPI

Miscellaneous Mississippi

Venues

W.C. Don's
P.O. Box 2464
Jackson, MS 39205
601-366-7371
Contact: Terry

Gin Restaurant
P.O. Box 1180
East Harrison Street
Oxford, MS 38655
601-234-0024
Contact: Mike Selaigman

Record Stores

Bebop Record Shop
900 East County Line Road
Unit 140
Ridgeland, MS 39157
601-981-5000
Contact: Ann Lampe

T E N N E S S E E

Memphis

Venues

Antenna
1588 Madison Ave.
Memphis, TN 38104
901-276-4052
Contact: Steve McGehee

Rum Boogie Cafe
182 Beale Street
Memphis, TN 38103
901-528-0150
Contact: Don McMinn
Blues

Record Stores

Boss Ugly Bob Records
726 East McLenore
Memphis, TN 38106
901-774-6400
Contact: Brandon or Bob

River Record
710 South Highland
Memphis, TN 38111
901-324-1757
Contact: Jerry Gibson

Radio Stations

WEVL
P.O. Box 40952
Memphis, TN 38174
901-278-3845

WKNO
P.O. Box 241880
Memphis, TN 38124-1880
901-458-2521

WLYX
Rhodes College
2000 North Pkwy.
Memphis, TN 38112
901-726-3735

Press

Malice
P.O. Box 241022
Memphis, TN 38124
901-682-1218
Contact: Chris Phinney
Quarterly fanzine

Nashville

Venues

Exit/In
2208 Elliston Place
Nashville, TN 37203
615-321-4400

Record Stores

Central Sound
3730 Vulcan Drive
Nashville, TN 37211
615-833-5960

Port O'Call Records
Harding Mall
4000 Nolensville Road
Nashville, TN 37211
615-833-0422
Contact: Kenny Warlick

Sam Goody's Records
2200 Elliston Place
Nashville, TN 37203
615-329-9727
Contact: Sheila Mann

Turtle's Records
2814 West End Road
Nashville, TN 37203
615-329-2287
Contact: Chip Hall

Radio Stations

WRVU
P.O. Box 9100
Nashville, TN 37235
615-322-3691

Miscellaneous Tennessee

Radio Stations

WAPX
Austin Peay State University
P.O. Box 4627
Clarksville, TN 37044
615-648-7200

WTTU
Tennessee Technological University
P.O. Box 5113
Cookeville, TN 38505
615-372-3688

WUTK
University of Tennessee
Andy Holt Tower
P103
Knoxville, TN 37996-0115
615-974-6897

WUTS
The University of the South
Student Post Office
Sewanee, TN 37375
615-598-1112

MID-ATLANTIC

- Maryland
- North Carolina
- South Carolina
- Virginia
- Washington, D.C.
- West Virginia

M A R Y L A N D

Annapolis

Record Stores

Record and Tape Exchange
901 Bay Ridge Road
Annapolis, MD 21403
301-267-0462
Contact: Anton Grobani

Radio Stations

WHFS
P.O. Box 829
Annapolis, MD 21404
301-261-2452

Baltimore

Venues

8 By 10
10 East Cross Street
Baltimore, MD 21230
301-625-2000

Hammerjacks
1101 South Howard Street
Baltimore, MD 21230
301-752-3302
Contact: Bud Becker

Radio Stations

WJHU
Johns Hopkins University
2216 North Charles Street
Baltimore, MD 21218
301-338-9548

College Park

Record Stores

Record and Tape Exchange
8608 Baltimore Blvd.
College Park, MD 20740
301-345-9338
Contact: Anton Grobani

Radio Stations

WMUC
University of Maryland
P.O. Box 99
College Park, MD 20742
301-454-3688, 301-454-2744

Hagarstown

Venues

Oliver's Pub
1565-67 Potomac Ave.
Hagarstown, MD 21740
301-790-0011
Contact: Dick
No country; mostly dance music

Radio Stations

WGTU
Route 9
P.O. 408A
Hagarstown, MD 21740
301-791-3690

Rockville

Record Stores

Olsson's Records
12350 Parklawn Drive
Rockville, MD 20852
301-338-6712
Contact: Elythia

Yesterday and Today Records
1327-J Rockville Pike
Rockville, MD 20852
301-279-7007
Contact: Dave Stimson

Radio Stations

WROC
Montgomery College
51 Mannakee Street
Rockville, MD 20850
301-279-5379

Silver Spring

Record Stores

Joe Lee's Record Paradise
2253 Bel-Pre Road
Silver Spring, MD 20906
301-598-8440
Contact: Joe Lee or Pat Carroll

Vinyl Ink Records
955 Bonifant
Silver Spring, MD 20910
301-58 Vinyl
Contact: George Gelestino

Radio Stations

WWDC
8750 Brookville Road
Silver Spring, MD 20910
301-587-7100

Miscellaneous Maryland

Record Stores

Kemp Mill Records
11420 Old Baltimore Place
Beltsville, MD 20705
301-595-9880
Contact: Lynn or Howard

Music Machine
1433 Reiserstown Road
Pikesville, MD 21208
301-633-0008

Phantasmagoria
11308 Grandview
Wheaton, MD 20902
301-949-8887
Contact: Bobby Rencher

Radio Stations

WSMC
St. Mary's College
St. Mary's, MD 20686
301-862-0214

WCVT
Towson State University
Media Center
Towson, MD 21204
301-321-2898, 301-321-2848

Press

Metropolitan Washington Ear
35 University Blvd. East
Silver Spring, MD 20901
301-681-6636
Contact: Kathie Kaelich

NORTH CAROLINA

North Carolina is a state people in the music business should not overlook. The middle of the state has four cities — Durham, Chapel Hill, Raleigh, and Greensboro — that have a concentrated university population. If a band or agent can hook up with the appropriate people in the area, a successful mini-tour can be arranged with minimal traveling expenses. Also, since a lot of students go back to their hometowns when school is in recess, radio play in this area can spread an artist's music effectively by concentrating promotion in this and other similar parts of the country.

Chapel Hill

Venues

Cat's Cradle
320 West Franklin
P.O. Box 351
Chapel Hill, NC 27514
919-967-6666
Contact: David, or Frank Heath

Record Stores

Schoolkids
144 East Franklin
Chapel Hill, NC 27514
919-929-7766
Contact: Andy

Radio Stations

WXYC
University of North Carolina-Chapel Hill
Carolina Union
P.O. Box 51
Chapel Hill, NC 27514
919-962-7768

Durham

Venues

Record Bar
33 Chapel Hill Blvd.
Durham, NC 27717
919-493-4511

Under the Street
1104 Broad Street
Durham, NC 27705
919-286-2647
Contact: Karl
All kinds of music

Record Stores

Poindexter Records
1916 Perry Street
Durham, NC 27705
919-286-1852
Contact: Jack Cambell

Record Bar
3333 Chapel Hill Blvd.
Durham, NC 27707
919-493-4511
Contact: Norman Hunter

Record Bar
1 Golden Drive
Durham, NC 27705
919-383-7473
Contact: Kevin Hawkins

Radio Stations

WXDU
Duke University
P.O. Box 4706
Durham, NC 27706
919-684-2957
Contact: Bryce Burkhardt
Station puts on monthly shows on campus coffeehouse — alternative and progressive music.

Greensboro

Venues

Nightshade Cafe, The
33 State Street
Greensboro, NC 27403
919-274-2019, 919-370-9177
Contact: Anelia
Blues and rock 'n' roll

Somewhere Else Tavern, The
2017 Freeman Mill Road
Greensboro, NC 27406
919-273-7532
Contact: Burley Hayes
Jam sessions on Sunday nights feature R & B, fusion, jazz, and any original music

Record Stores

Record Exchange
340 Tate Street
Greensboro, NC 27403
919-274-2300
Contact: Pete

Schoolkids Records
1600 Spring Garden
Greensboro, NC 27403
919-275-1226
Contact: John Stevenson

Radio Stations

WQFS
Guilford College
P.O. Box 17714
Greensboro, NC 27410
919-294-3820

WUAG
University of North Carolina
Elliot Center 26
100 Spring Garden Street
Greensboro, NC 27412
919-334-5470

Raleigh

Venues

Brewery, The
5 West Hargett Street
Raleigh, NC 27601
919-834-5977
Bookings: Black Park Management
Contact: Ed Morgan, Kenny Hobby, or Jordon Lea
Progressive and reggae

Fallout Shelter, The
2 South West Street
Raleigh, NC 27603
919-832-8855
Contact: Scott, Steve, or Eric

Record Stores

Oasis Records
2316 Hillsborough Street, Suite 104
Raleigh, NC 27607
919-821-7766
Contact: Kim or Greg

Radio Stations

WKNC
North Carolina State University
P.O. Box 8607
Raleigh, NC 27695-8607
919-737-2400

Press

Spectator Magazine
P.O. Box 12887
Raleigh, NC 27605
919-828-7393
Contact: Godfrey Cheshire, Music Editor

Miscellaneous North Carolina

Venues

Double Door
218 Independence Blvd.
Charlotte, NC 28204
704-376-1446
Contact: Nick

Record Stores

Record and Tape Depot
103 East King Street
Boone, NC 28608
704-264-7168
Contact: Scott Whipple

Selector Records
2126 Hgwy. 70 Southeast
Hickory, NC 28602
704-322-6002
Contact: Susan Haynes

Radio Stations

WCQS
73 Broadway
Ashville, NC 28801
704-253-6875

WDAV
Davidson College
P.O. Box 1540
Davidson, NC 28036
704-892-8900

WOSE
Elon College
P.O. Box 6000
Elon College, NC 27244
919-584-2574

WZMB
E.C.U.
Second Floor, Old Joyner Library
Greenville, NC 27834
919-757-6656

WSAP
St. Andrews Presbyterian College
Communications Office
Laurenburg, NC 28352
919-276-3652, X380

WLOZ
University of North Carolina-
Wilmington
601 South College Road
Wilmington, NC 28403
919-395-3086

WAKE
Wake Forest University
P.O. Box 7760
Reynolds Station
Winston-Salem, NC 27109
919-761-5129

S O U T H   C A R O L I N A

Columbia

Venues

Green Street
1101 Harden Street
Columbia, SC 29205
803-779-8252
Contact: Doug Goalsby

Rockefellers
2112 Divine Street
Columbia, SC 29205
803-252-7625
Contact: Art Borke
All kinds of music

Record Stores

Manifest Records
1932 Main Street
Columbia, SC 29201
803-256-2606
Contact: Donna Maxwell

Radio Stations

WKWQ
712 Richland, Suite F
Columbia, SC 29201
803-779-1095

WLTR
2901 Millwood Ave.
Columbia, SC 29205
803-737-3420

WUSC
University of South Carolina
Drawer B
Columbia, SC 29208
803-777-7172

Press

GameCock
Drawer A
Russell House
University of South Carolina
Columbia, SC 29208
803-777-7181
Contact: Todd Hines

Greenville

Venues

Studio B Lounge
1243 South Pleasantburg Drive
Greenville, SC 29605
803-277-9096
Contact: Lois Blackwelder

Radio Stations

WPLS
Furman University
P.O. Box 28573
Greenville, SC 29613
803-294-2757

Press

Greenville News
P.O. Box 1688
Greenville, SC 29602
803-298-4315
Contact: Lynn P. Lucas

Miscellaneous South Carolina

Venues

Windjammer
1008 Ocean Blvd.
Isle of Palms, SC 29451
803-886-8596
Contact: Bobby Ross

After Deck
P.O. Box 3380
Myrtle Beach, SC 29577
803-449-1550
Contact: Bill Rippy

Radio Stations

WSBF
Clemson University
P.O. Box 9260
Clemson, SC 29632
803-656-4010

WSCI
P.O. Box 801
Mount Pleasant, SC 29464
803-881-1160

V I R G I N I A

Blacksburg

Venues

South Main Cafe
117 South Main Street
Blacksburg, VA 24060
703-382-8370, 703-951-8202
Contact: Linda Schwab
Any kind of music

Record Stores

Books, Strings and Things
214 Draper Road
Blacksburg, VA 24060
703-552-8633
Contact: Kurt or Randall

Record Exchange
322 North Main Street
Blacksburg, VA 24060
703-961-2500
Contact: Rick McCrickard

Radio Stations

WUVT
Virginia Polytechnic Institute
100 North Main Street, Suite 210
Blacksburg, VA 24060
703-951-1642

Charlottesville
Venues

Mine Shaft
1107 West Main Street
Charlottesville, VA 22903
804-977-6656
Contact: Rising Tide Productions
P.O. Box 1902
Charlottesville, VA 22903
804-979-4842
Al Hinton or Chris Munson
Any kind of music

Record Stores

Back Alley Discs
904 West Main Street
Charlottesville, VA 22903
804-977-0110
Contact: Bruce Rogers

Disc Traxshuns
Seminole Square Shopping Center
Charlottesville, VA 22903
804-973-7060
Contact: Bruce Rogers

Radio Stations

WTJU
University of Virginia
711 Newcomb Hall Station
Charlottesville, VA 22901
804-924-3418

WUVA
Station 1
Charlottesville, VA 22904
804-924-3194

Fairfax
Record Stores

Penguin Feather Records
10967 Lee Hgwy.
Fairfax, VA 22030
703-385-2110
Indy Buyer

Radio Stations

WGMU
George Mason University
4400 University Drive
Fairfax, VA 22153
703-323-3542

Harrisonburg
Venues

Mystic Den
29 South Liberty Street
Harrisonburg, VA 22801
703-434-8706
Contact: Debbie Anderson
All college bands

Press

Breeze
Anthony Seeger Hall
James Madison University
Harrisonburg, VA 22807
703-568-6127
Contact: Laura Hunt
College newspaper

Richmond

Venues

Flood Zone
P.O. Box 7105
11 South 18th Street
Richmond, VA 23221
804-644-0935
Contact: Steve Payne
All kinds of music

New Horizon Cafe
1203 West Broad
Richmond, VA 23220
804-353-4743
Contact: James Barber
International and reggae

Record Stores

Gary's Records
6017 West Broad Street
Richmond, VA 23230
804-288-1945
Contact: Robert Gary

Plan Nine Records
3002 West Cary Street
Richmond, VA 23221
804-353-9996
Contact: Bob Schick

Radio Stations

WVCW
Virginia Commonwealth College
916 West Franklin Street
Richmond, VA 23220
804-367-1057

Press

Style Weekly
1000 West Franklin Street
Richmond, VA 23220
804-358-0825

Miscellaneous Virginia

Venues

Bayou
C/O Cellar Door Productions
329 South Patrick
Alexandria, VA 22314
703-683-1900
Contact: Bill
All kinds of music

Gerald's
1324 King Street
Alexandria, VA 22314
703-836-7866
Contact: Gerald Terlitzki
Original music

Luckies
1033 Norwood Street
Radford, VA 24141
703-731-1902
Contact: Don Whitesell
Great club, even has its own newspaper. Progressive, R & B, and classic. No heavy metal.

Record Stores

Books, Strings and Things
202 Market Square
Roanoke, VA 24011
703-342-5590
Contact: Mike Waoke

Electric Smiles/Records
101 South Witchduck Road
Virginia Beach, VA 23452
804-456-0695
Contact: Mike

Radio Stations

WVVV
P.O. Box 30
Christiansburg, VA 24073
703-382-4993

WLUR
Washington & Lee University
Lexington, VA 24450
703-463-8443

WHRO
5200 Hampton Blvd.
Norfolk, VA 23508
804-489-9484

WNOR
801 Boush Street
Norfolk, VA 23510
804-623-9667

WODU
Old Dominion University
Webb Center, Room 201
Norfolk, VA 23529
804-683-3441

WCWM
College of William & Mary
Campus Center
Williamsburg, VA 23185
804-229-2600

W A S H I N G T O N, D. C.

Our capital has a happening underground scene, considering the conservative administration it houses.

Venues

9:30 Club
930 F Street Northwest
Washington, D.C., 20004
202-638-2008
Contact: Holly Meyers
Alternative and progressive

DC Space
443 Seventh Street Northwest
Washington, D.C., 20004
202-393-0255
Contact: Cynthia
Small but has diverse following

East Side
1824 Half Street Southwest
Washington, D.C., 20024
202-488-1205
Contact: Terry Folks

Grog and Tankard
2408 Wisconsin Ave. Northwest
Washington, D.C., 20007
202-333-3114
Contact: Abdul
R & B, classics, progressive and rock 'n' roll. No country, metal, or punk.

Record Stores

Olsson's Records
1307 19th Street Northwest
Washington, D.C., 20036
202-785-2662
Contact: Brooke Higdon

Olsson's Records
1900 L Street Northwest
Washington, D.C., 20036
202-785-5037
Indy Buyer

Olsson's Records
1239 Wisconsin Ave. Northwest
Washington, D.C., 20007
202-338-6712
Contact: Brian McGuire

Smash Records
3324 M Street Northwest
Washington, D.C., 20007
202-337-6274
Contact: Bobby

Tower Records
2000 Pennsylvania Ave. Northwest
Washington, D.C., 20006
202-331-2400
Indy Buyer

Vexie Maxie's Records
5772 Second Street Northeast
Washington, D.C., 20011
202-269-6260
Contact: Phil McConnell
Main office for 29 stores

Radio Stations

WCUA
Catholic University
P.O. Box 184
Cardinal Station
Washington, D.C., 20064
202-635-5106

WDCU
4200 Connecticut Northwest
Washington, D.C., 20008
202-282-7588

WDJY
5321 First Place Northeast
Washington, D.C., 20011
202-722-1000

WETA
P.O. Box 2626
Washington, D.C., 20013
703-998-2790

WGTB
SAC Office
316 Leavey Center
Georgetown University
Washington, D.C., 20057
202-687-3701

WHUR
529 Bryant Street Northwest
Washington, D.C., 20059
202-232-6000

WPFW
702 H Street Northwest
Washington, D.C., 20001
202-783-3100

WVAU
American University
P.O. Box 610
Washington, D.C., 20016
202-885-6161

Press

City Paper
724 Ninth Street Northwest, Suite 500
Washington, D.C., 20001
202-628-6528
Contact: Alona Wartofsky, Music Editor

Washington Times
3600 New York Ave. Northeast
Washington, D.C., 20002
202-636-3000
Contact: Octavia Roca

WEST VIRGINIA

Morgantown

"The nicest, most honest people in the music business in the most out-of-the way place on earth."
—Stephen Marsh from Miracle Room

Venues

Underground Railroad
123 Pleasant Street
Morgantown, WV 26505
304-291-6994
Contact: Michelle
Everything but disco or polka

Record Stores

Backstreet Records
370 High Street
Morgantown, WV 26505
304-296-3203
Contact: Eric Hansmann or Mark Bell

Record Bar
Mountaineer Mall, Hgwy. 73 and Greenback Road
Morgantown, WV 26505
304-296-6194
Contact: Jamie Ford

Radio Stations

WWVU
West Virginia University
Mountainlair
Morgantown, WV 26506
304-293-3329

Press

Daily Anthem Paper
284 Prospect Street
Morgantown, WV 26506
304-293-4141
Contact: Rick Smith
University paper

Miscellaneous West Virginia

Radio Stations

WVBC
Bethany College
Bethany, WV 26032
304-829-7562

Network of 8 Public Stations
West Virginia Broadcasting
600 Capitol Street
Charleston, WV 25301
304-348-3421

WMUL
Marshall University
900 Halgreer Blvd.
Huntington, WV 25755
304-696-2295

WUIS
West Virginia State College
P.O. Box 31
Institute, WV 25112
304-766-8526

WKLC
100 Kanawha Terrace
St. Albans, WV 25177
304-722-3300

AROUND
NEW YORK

- New Jersey
- New York
- Pennsylvania

NEW JERSEY

Asbury Park

Bruce Springsteen territory.

Venues

Stone Pony
913 Ocean Ave.
Asbury Park, NJ 07712
201-988-7177, 201-988-7267
Contact: Mr. Pieoka
Rock 'n' roll

Radio Stations

WHTG
1129 Hope Road
Asbury Park, NJ 07712
201-542-1410

Dover

Venues

Showplace
347 South Salem Street
Dover, NJ 07801
201-361-6460
Contact: Larry Gribler

Radio Stations

WDHA
419 State Hgwy. 10
Dover, NJ 07801
201-328-1055

Hoboken

Venues

Maxwell's
1039 Washington
Hoboken, NJ 07030
201-656-9632
Contact: Todd Abramson

Record Stores

Pier Platter Records
56 Newark Street
Hoboken, NJ 07030
201-795-4785, 201-795-9015
Contact: Tom

Radio Stations

WCPR
Stevens Technology
P.O. Box 1461
Castle Point Station
Hoboken, NJ 07030
201-795-4887

Press

Breakthrough
P.O. Box 1123
Hoboken, NJ 07030
201-659-2461
Contact: Todd Abramson

Hudson Reporter, The
1321 Washington Street
Hoboken, NJ 07030
201-798-7800
Contact: Craig Winkoman

Montclair

Record Stores

Crazy Rhythms
561 Bloomfield Ave.
Montclair, NJ 07042
201-744-5787
Contact: Joseph Provenzano

Radio Stations

WMSC
Room 110 Student Center Annex
Montclair State College
Montclair, NJ 07043
201-893-7466

Neptune

Venues

Green Parrot
1927 Hgwy. 33
Neptune, NJ 07753
201-775-1991
Contact: Tom
Original rock 'n' roll

Press

Asbury Park Press
3601 Hgwy. 66
P.O. Box 1550
Neptune, NJ 07754
201-922-6000
Contact: Gretchen Van Benthuysen

New Brunswick

Venues

Court Tavern
124 Church Street
New Brunswick, NJ 08901
201-545-7265
Contact: Cathy or Tom

Music in a Different Kitchen
29 Easton Ave.
New Brunswick, NJ 08901
201-545-3551
Contact: Judy Mallen

Record Stores

Cheap Thrills
382 George Street
New Brunswick, NJ 08901
201-246-2422
Contact: Cathy or Yuri

Hot Tracks
116 Somerset Street
New Brunswick, NJ 08901
201-246-8057
Contact: Dennis Mentzel

Radio Stations

WRSU
Rutgers University Student Center
126 College Ave.
New Brunswick, NJ 08903
201-932-8800

Princeton

Venues

Terrace Club
62 Washington Road
Princeton, NJ 08540
609-924-6095
Contact: Nisid
*All kinds of music, especially radical or
hard core*

Campus Club
5 Prospect Street
Princeton, NJ 08540
609-924-5122
Contact: Sebastian Hardy
Rock 'n' roll

Record Stores

Princeton Record Exchange
20 South Tulane Street
Princeton, NJ 08542
609-921-0881
Contact: Brian Dornbach

Radio Stations

WPRB
Princeton University
Holder Hall
P.O. Box 342
Princeton, NJ 08540
609-921-9284

Miscellaneous New Jersey

Venues

Dirt Club
10 Orange Street
Bloomfield, NJ 07003
201-748-6474
Contact: Johnny Dirt
Original music

Loop Lounge
373 Broadway
Passaic, NJ 07055
201-365-0807
Contact: Bruce
Original rock 'n' roll

Record Stores

Wall to Wall Sound
200 South Route 130
Cinnaminson, NJ 08077
609-829-4030
Indy Buyer

Vintage Vinyl Record
Lafayette Road
Fords, NJ 08863
201-225-7717
Contact: Rob Roth

Radio Stations

WRCB
Rutgers
Camden College Center
Fourth and Penn Street
Camden, NJ 08102
609-757-6418

WGLS
Glassboro State College
Glassboro, NJ 08028
609-863-7336, 609-863-7335

WNTI
Centenary College
400 Jefferson Street
Hackettstown, NJ 07840
201-852-4545

WWRC
Rider College
P.O. Box 6400
2083 Lawrenceville Road
Lawrenceville, NJ 08648
609-896-5211

WBJB
Brookdale Community College
Lincroft, NJ 07738
201-842-1827

135

WFDM
Fairleigh Dickenson University
285 Madison Ave.
Madison, NJ 07940
201-593-8585

WMNJ
Drew University
36 Madison Ave.
Madison, NJ 07940
201-408-3000
Contact: Mr. Jaime Lavender, Public Service Director

WRPR
505 Ramapo Valley Road
Mahwah, NJ 07430
201-825-1234

WACC
Atlantic Community College
Room 322
May's Landing, NJ 08330
609-343-5240

WBGO
54 Park Place
Newark, NJ 07102
201-624-8880

WRNU
Rutgers University
350 Martin Luther King Drive
Newark, NJ 07102
201-648-5187

WBCC
Bergen Community College
400 Paramus Road
Paramus, NJ 07652
201-447-9240

WLFR
Stockton State College
Pomona, NJ 08240
609-652-4917, 609-652-4780

WCCM
City College of Morris
Route 10 and Center Grove Road
Randolph, NJ 07801
201-361-9886

WFDU
Fairleigh Dickenson University
795 Cedar Lane
Teaneck, NJ 07666
201-692-2806

WTSR
Trenton State College
Kendall Hall
Trenton, NJ 08625
609-771-2420
Contact: Doris Duwe

WOCC
Ocean City Community College
2001 CN College Drive
Toms River, NJ 08753
201-255-0400, X2135

WPSC
William Paterson State College
300 Pompton Road
Hobert Hall
Wayne, NJ 07474
201-595-3331

Press

Earwax
444 Ringwood Ave.
Wannaque, NJ 07465
201-839-6020
Contact: Harry Baggs
Fanzine

Making Tyme
131 West Passaic Street
P.O. Box 100A
Maywood, NJ 07607
201-845-7032
Contact: Mick London
Bi-monthly fanzine

NEW YORK

Albany

Venues

Polly's Hotel
337 Central Ave.
Albany, NY 12205
518-465-7423
Contact: Don Dwarkin or John Wasniewski, DDE Music Management
P.O. Box 457
Albany, NY 12201
R & B, roots rock and reggae

QE2
280 Lark Street
Albany, NY 12210
518-434-2697
Contact: Charlene Shortsleeve
12 Central Ave.
Albany, NY 12210
518-434-2697

Record Stores

Erl Records
418 Madison Ave.
Albany, NY 12210
518-432-0851
Contact: Dave

Music Shack
65 Central Ave.
Albany, NY 12206
518-436-4581
Contact: Rocky Roy

Record Town, Inc.
20 Wolf Road
Albany, NY 12205
518-459-6247
Indy Buyer

Records N Such
Stuyvesant Plaza
Albany, NY 12203
518-438-3003
Indy Buyer

Sunytunes
Campus Center
1400 Washington Ave.
Albany, NY 12222
518-442-3300
Indy Buyer

World's Records
132 Central Ave.
Albany, NY 12206
518-462-5271
Contact: Frank Lafalce

Radio Stations

WCDB
State University of New York
Campus Center 316
1400 Washington Ave.
Albany, NY 12222
518-442-5262

WQBK
P.O. Box 1300
Albany, NY 12201
518-462-5555

Press

Buzz
P.O. Box 3111
Albany, NY 12203
518-489-0658
Contact: George Guarino, Publisher/Editor
Monthly publication

Buffalo

Venues

Mr. Goodbar
1110 Elmwood Ave.
Buffalo, NY 14222
716-886-9178
Contact: Art Ponto
A lot of new music, open to many styles, especially old rock and jazz

Nietzchies
248 Allen Street
Buffalo, NY 14201
716-886-8539
Contact: Joe Rubino
Jazz, blues, reggae, and contemporary rock

Record Stores

Doris Records
286 East Ferry Street
Buffalo, NY 14208
716-883-2410
Indy Buyer

Home of the Hits
1105 Elmwood Ave.
Buffalo, NY 14222
716-883-0330
Contact: Jennifer Flynn

Record Mine
3048 Delaware Ave.
Buffalo, NY 14217
716-874-6538
Indy Buyer

Record Theater
1800 Main Street
Buffalo, NY 14208
716-883-9520
Contact: Jim Primerano

Ruda's Record Shoppe
915 Broadway Ave.
Buffalo, NY 14212
716-852-3121
Contact: Don Ruda

Radio Stations

WBFO
State University of New York-Buffalo
Second Floor Allen Hall
3435 Main Street
Buffalo, NY 14214
716-831-2555

WBNY
1300 Elmwood Ave.
Buffalo, NY 14222
716-878-5104

WNCB
Medaille College
18 Agassiz Circle
Buffalo, NY 14214
716-884-3281, X222

Press

Buffalo News
P.O. Box 100
1 News Plaza
Buffalo, NY 14240
716-849-3434
Contact: Dale Anderson

Free Times
257 Elmwood Ave.
Buffalo, NY 14222
716-882-4455

Ithaca
Venues

Haunt
404 South Albany
Ithaca, NY 14580
607-273-3355, 607-273-7677
Contact: John Peterson,
212-529-7218

Record Stores

Jazz Plus
130 Fayette Street
Ithaca, NY 14850
607-272-7436
Contact: Eddie B. Smith

Rebop Records
409 College Ave.
Ithaca, NY 14850
607-273-0737
Contact: Bob, or Renee Baum

Radio Stations

WICB
Ithaca College
Hannah Broadcast Center
Ithaca, NY 14850
607-274-3217

WVBR
Cornell University
227 Linden Ave.
Ithaca, NY 14850
607-273-4000

Press

Grapevine Press
108 South Albany Street
Ithaca, NY 14850
607-272-3470

Ithaca Times
P.O. Box 27
Ithaca, NY 14851
607-273-6092
Contact: Sandy List

Latham
Record Stores

Clark Music
1075 Troy-Schenectady Road
Latham, NY 12110
518-785-4322
Contact: Rick Rowley

Radio Stations

WPYX
1054 Troy-Schenectady Road
Latham, NY 12110
518-785-9061

New York City
Venues

Bedrock
316 West 49th Street
New York, NY 10019
212-246-8976
Contact: Marty

Bitter End
147 Bleeker Street
New York, NY 10002
212-673-7030
Contact: Ken Gorka
All kinds of music

Bottom Line
15 West Fourth Street
New York, NY 10012
212-228-6300
Contact: Donna or Alan
Big stars

Cat Club
76 East 13th Street
New York, NY 10003
212-505-0090
Contact: Tommy Gunn
Rock 'n' roll

CBGB's and OMFUG
315 Bowery
New York, NY 10003
212-982-4052
Contact: Louise
All kinds of music

China Club
2130 Broadway
New York, NY 10023
212-877-1166
Contact: Tommy Allen
Rock 'n' roll

Downtown Beruit
158 First Ave.
New York, NY 10009
212-260-4248

Kenny's Castaway
157 Bleeker
New York, NY 10012
212-473-9870
Contact: Roger Probert
Leans toward rock 'n' roll but will consider any music

Knitting Factory
47 East Houston
New York, NY 10012
212-219-3006
Contact: Mike Dorf
Any kind of music

Limelight
47 West 20th Street
New York, NY 10011
212-807-7850
All kinds of music, especially metal

Lismar Lounge
41 East First Ave.
New York, NY 10003
212-777-9477
Contact: Roger
Rock 'n' roll

Lone Star Cafe
61 Fifth Ave.
New York, NY 10003
212-242-1664
Contact: Mark Krantz
Not much jazz or heavy metal but almost everything else

Nirvana Club One
1 Times Square Plaza
New York, NY 10036
212-486-6868

Octagon
555 West 33rd Street
New York, NY 10001
212-947-0400
Contact: Seth Hyman

Palladium
123 East 13th Street
New York, NY 10003
212-473-7171
Contact: Ron Pelsner
212-249-7773
Rock 'n' roll

Pyramid Club
101 Avenue A
New York, NY 10003
212-420-1590
Contact: Brian or Allen

Ritz, The
119 East 11th Street
New York, NY 10003
212-529-5295
Contact: Chuck Beardsly
Big names, booked through Monarch Entertainment
P.O. Box 1566
Montclair, NJ 07042
201-744-0770

Tunnel, The
220 12th Ave. at 27th Street
New York, NY 10001
212-244-6444
Contact: Ann Morin
Any kind of music

World Club
254 East Second Street
New York, NY 10003
212-477-8677
Contact: Steven Irwin
All kinds of music

Record Stores

34th Street Records
367 West 34th Street
New York, NY 10001
212-736-2795
Contact: Max Draisner

Bleeker Bob's
118 West Third Street
New York, NY 10012
212-475-9677
Contact: Craig

Bondy's Records
38 Park Row
New York, NY 10038
212-964-5886
Contact: Marie Rodriquez

CBGB Record Canteen
313 Bowery
New York, NY 10003
212-677-0455
Contact: Ned Hayden

Chin Randy's Records
1342 St. Johns Place
Brooklyn, NY 11213
718-778-9470
Contact: Victor Chin

Disc O Mat
474 Seventh Ave.
New York, NY 10018
212-736-1150
Contact: Jerry Polito

Finyl Vinyl
89 Second Ave.
New York, NY 10003
212-533-8007
Contact: Robert or Irwin

Freebeing Records
52 Carmine Street
New York, NY 10014
Contact: by mail

Golden Disc
239 Bleeker Street
New York, NY 10014
212-255-7899
Contact: David G.

Hideout Records
5 Cornelia St.
New York, NY 10014
212-463-8900
Contact: Michael

Irie-Ites
112 East Seventh Street
New York, NY 10009
212-529-3855
Contact: Catherine Tobias

Midnight Records
255 West 23rd Street
P.O. Box 390
Old Chelsea Station
New York, NY 10011
212-675-2768
Indy Buyer

Moodie's Records
3976 White Plains Road
Bronx, NY 10466
212-654-8368
Contact: Howard

Record Factory
17 West Eighth Street
New York, NY 10011
212-228-4800
Contact: Victor Degro

Rocks in Your Head
157 Prince Street
New York, NY 10012
212-475-6934
Contact: Ira

Second Coming Records
235 Sullivan
New York, NY 10012
212-228-1313
Contact: Ewa

Sounds
20 St. Marks Place
New York, NY 10003
212-677-3444
Contact: Joe

Tower Records
692 Broadway
New York, NY 10012
212-505-1500

Tower Records
1961 Broadway
New York, NY 10023
212-799-2500
Indy Buyer

Venus Records
61 West Eighth Street
New York, NY 10011
212-598-4459, 212-598-9755
Contact: Bill Shore

Wiz, The
2488-92 Flatbush
Brooklyn, NY 11234
718-252-3700
Indy Buyer

Radio Stations

WBMB
Baruch College
155 East 24th Street
New York, NY 10010
212-725-7168

WBRC
Brooklyn College of the Arts
City University of New York
Brooklyn, NY 11210
718-780-5589

WCCR
City University of New York
Finley Student Center
133rd & Convent Ave.
New York, NY 10031
212-690-8171

WFUV
Fordham University
Bronx, NY 10458
212-365-8056, 212-365-8050

WHBI
477 82nd Street
Brooklyn, NY 11209
718-745-2537

WKCR
Columbia University
208 Ferris Booth Hall
New York, NY 10027
212-854-5223

WKRB
2001 Oriental Blvd.
Brooklyn, NY 11235
718-934-9572

WNEW-FM
655 Third Ave.
New York, NY 10017
212-986-7000, 212-286-1027

WNWK
515 Madison Ave.
Room 1303
New York, NY 10022
212-826-1059

WNYC
1 Centre Street
New York, NY 10007
212-669-7800

WNYU
721 Broadway
11th Floor
New York, NY 10003
212-998-1660

WTNY
New York Institute of Technology
1855 Broadway
New York, NY 10031
212-757-7121

Press

Ear Magazine
325 Spring Street
Room 208
New York, NY 10013
212-807-7944
Contact: David Laskin

New Route, The
114 East 28th Street
Suite 400
New York, NY 10016
212-481-1010
Contact: Doug Joseph

New York Native
P.O. Box 1475
Church Street Station
New York, NY 10008
212-627-2120
Contact: Cliff Schwartz

New York Times
229 West 43rd Street
New York, NY 10036
212-556-1234

Newsday New York
780 Third Ave.
New York, NY 10017
212-303-2800
Contact: Caroline Miller

People Magazine
C/O Time Inc.
Time Life Building
Rockefeller Plaza
New York, NY 10020
212-522-1212
Contact: Cutler Durkee

Reflex Magazine
120 East 32nd Street, Suite 40T
New York, NY 10016
212-532-9858
Contact: Rich Shupe

Village Voice
842 Broadway
New York, NY 10003
212-475-3300

Oneonta

Record Stores

Village Music
116 Main Street
Oneonta, NY 13820
607-432-7055
Contact: Nick or Suzanne

WRHO
Communications Center
Hartwick College
Oneonta, NY 13820
607-432-3262

Radio Stations

WONY
State College-Oneonta
Alumni Hall
Oneonta, NY 13802
607-431-2712

Port Chester

Venues

Marty's
107 Adee Street
Port Chester, NY 10573
914-939-9545
Contact: Marty Junior

Record Stores

Vinyl Solution
109 Adee Street
Port Chester, NY 10573
914-939-5769
Contact: Jeff Loh

Poughkeepsie

Record Stores

Book and Record
Commerce Street
Poughkeepsie, NY 12603
914-229-5505
Contact: Lou Kustas

WVKR
Vassar College
P.O. Box 166
Poughkeepsie, NY 12601
914-473-5866

Radio Stations

WMCR
Marist College
82 North Road
Poughkeepsie, NY 12601
914-471-3240, X132

Rochester

Venues

Backstreets
14 Charlotte Street
Rochester, NY 14607
716-454-2392
Contact: Paul
Any kind of music

Idols
88 Liberty Pole Way
Rochester, NY 14604
716-232-3410
Contact: Richard Kaza
Progressive, alternative, and other types of music

Jazzberry's
715 Monroe Ave.
Rochester, NY 14607
716-262-3660

Red Crook Inn
300 Jefferson Road
Rochester, NY 14623
716-424-1760
Contact: Jeff Springut
All types of music

Rumor's Nightclub
670 South Ave.
Rochester, NY 14620
716-271-6405

Record Stores

Bop Shop, The
274 North Goodman Street
Village Gate Square
Rochester, NY 14607
716-271-3354
Contact: Tom Kohn

House of Guitars
645 Titus Ave.
Rochester, NY 14617
716-544-9928
Contact: Tom

Lakeshore Record Exchange
4410 Lake Ave.
Rochester, NY 14602
716-663-1447
Contact: Andrew Chinnici

Record Archive, Inc.
1394 Mount Hope Ave.
Rochester, NY 14620
716-473-3820
Contact: Jim Huey or Alayna Hill

Record Time
673 Monroe Ave.
Rochester, NY 14607
716-442-1150
Contact: Dave Senior

Radio Stations

WIRQ
260 Cooper Road
Rochester, NY 14617
716-342-6461

WITR
Institute of Technology
P.O. Box 9969
Rochester, NY 14623
716-475-2000

WJFC
St. John Fisher College
3690 East Ave.
Rochester, NY 14618
716-385-8000

WMCC
Monroe Community College
100 East Henrietta Road
Rochester, NY 14623
716-424-5200

WRUR
Todd Union Hall
Rochester, NY 14627
716-275-5966

WSCX
St. John Fisher College
3690 East Ave.
Rochester, NY 14618
716-385-8176

Press

Free Time
850 University Ave.
Rochester, NY 14607
716-473-2266
Contact: Sue Cannon
Very good bi-weekly, including full music section

Saratoga Springs

Venues

Metro Cafe
17 Maple Ave.
Saratoga Springs, NY 12866
518-584-9581
All bookings by DDE Music Management

Record Stores

The Disc Line
40 Caroline Street
Saratoga Springs, NY 12866
518-583-0311

Radio Stations

WSPN
Skidmore College
Saratoga Springs, NY 12866
518-584-7378

Schenectady

Record Stores

Up Your Alley
133 Jay Street
Schenectady, NY 12305
518-381-6166
Contact: Dave Clayton

Radio Stations

WRUC
College Center/Union College
Schenectady, NY 12308
518-370-6151

Syracuse

Venues

Lost Horizon
5863 Thompson
Syracuse, NY 13214
315-446-1934
Contact: Greg Itialiano
All kinds of music, especially metal and rock 'n' roll

Press

Syracuse New Times
1415 West Genesee Street
Syracuse, NY 13204
315-422-7011
Contact: Russ Tarby

Troy

Record Stores

Music Shack
295 River Street
Troy, NY 12180
518-273-1400
Contact: Don Roy

Radio Stations

WRPI
Rennsselaer Polytech Institute
1 WRPI Plaza
Troy, NY 12181
518-276-6636

Miscellaneous New York

Venues

Hawthorne Inn
408 Elwood
Hawthorne, NY 10592
914-769-9655
Contact: Talent Connection
914-667-4353
All types of music

Casablanca
125 White Spruce Blvd.
Henrietta, NY 14683
716-424-5096

Bendover's
600 Fifth Ave.
Pelham, NY 10803
914-738-9753
Contact: Donny
All music except heavy metal

Record Stores

Cavages, Inc., Record Department
Boulevard Mall
Amherst, NY 14222
716-836-4482
Contact: Mark Wochadlo

Chaffee Sound and Electronics
Route 16
Chaffee, NY 14030
716-496-7216
Contact: Roger Garbowski

Record Giant
D and F Plaza
Dunkirk, NY 14048
716-366-5201
Contact: Fran

The Record Stop
Main Street
Eastport, NY 11941
516-325-1249
Indy Buyer

P and Jay's Harbor Sounds Ltd.
109 Main Street
Point Jefferson, NY 11777
516-928-3036

The Record Stop
130 East Main Street
Riverhead, NY 11901
516-727-7789
Contact: Bruce Berg

The Record Stop
279 Portion Road
Ronkonkoma, NY 11779
516-585-3294
Contact: Bruce Berg

Slipped Disc Records
68 Rockway Ave.
Valley Stream, NY 11580
516-872-0516
Contact: Debbie or Mike

Cavages, Inc., Record Department
Seneca Mall
Ridge & Slade Ave.
West Seneca, NY 14224
716-823-1332

New World Records
410 Evans Street
Williamsville, NY 14221
716-634-4004
Contact: Chris Madden

Radio Stations

WALF
Alfred University
P.O. Box 548
Alfred, NY 14802
607-871-2200

WHRW-FM
State University of New York-
Binghamton
Binghamton, NY 13901
607-798-2139

WBSU
State University of New York-
Brockport
Seymour College Union
Brockport, NY 14420
716-395-2500

WCWP
Long Island University
Post Campus
Brookville, NY 11548
516-299-2626

KSLU
St. Lawrence University
Canton, NY 13617
315-379-5257

WCIR
New York Institute of Technology
Central Islip
Central Islip, NY 11722
516-348-3237

WHCL
Hamilton College
P.O. Box 82
Clinton, NY 13323
315-859-7200, 315-859-4200

WCEB
Corning Community College
Spencer Hill Road
P.O. Box 200
Corning, NY 14830
607-962-9360

WSUC
State University of New York-
Cortland
Brockway Hall
Cortland, NY 13045
607-753-2936

WTBQ
62 North Main
Florida, NY 10921
914-651-4446

WCVF
State University of New York-
Fredonia
109 Gregory Hall
Fredonia, NY 14063
716-673-3420

WBAU AM/FM
P.O. Box 365
Garden City, NY 11530
516-747-4757

WGSU
State University of New York-
Geneseo
Geneseo, NY 14454
716-245-5586

WEOS
Echo of the Seneca
Geneva, NY 14456
315-789-8970

WRCU
Colgate University
Hamilton, NY 13346
315-824-1212

WKJY
384 Clinton Street
Hempstead, NY 11550
516-481-8000

WRHU
Hofstra University
Hempstead, NY 11550
516-560-5667

WRNP
College at New Paltz
Student Union 413
New Paltz, NY 12561
914-257-3070

WICR
715 North Ave.
New Rochelle, NY 10801
914-633-2369

WGMC
P.O. Box 300
North Greece, NY 14515
716-225-5330

WNYT
New York Institute of Technology
P.O. Box 429
Old Westbury, NY 11568
516-626-3780

WOCR
State University of New York
Hewitt Union
Oswego, NY 13126
315-341-2101

WBER
2596 Baird Road
Penfield, NY 14526
716-381-4353

WPLT
State University of New York-
Plattsburgh
Office of Campus Life
Plattsburgh, NY 12901
518-564-2727

WRPW
Pace University
861 Bedford Road
Pleasantville, NY 10570
914-741-3703

WTSC
Clarkson College
Potsdam, NY 13676
315-265-7180

WPUR
State University of New York
Purchase, NY 10577
914-253-6984

WRCN
P.O. Box 666
Riverhead, NY 11901
516-727-1570

WSBU
St. Bonaventure University
P.O. Box 0
St. Bonaventure, NY 14778
716-375-2307, 716-375-2306

WHSE
Smithtown High School East
34 Spring Hollow Road
St. James, NY 11780
516-862-7419

WPBX
Southhampton College
Southhampton, NY 11968
516-283-4000, X290

WSIA
College of Staten Island
715 Ocean Terrace
Staten Island, NY 10301
718-448-9742

WUSB
State University of New York-
Stonybrook
Student Union Building
Stonybrook, NY 11794
516-632-6500

WKWZ
Syosset High School
Southwoods Road
Syosset, NY 11791
516-921-8850

WPNR
Utica College
Burrstone Road
Utica, NY 13502
315-792-3069

WARY
P.O. Box 258
Valhalla, NY 10595
914-285-6752
Contact: Jim Gibson, Music Director

WNGZ
421 North Franklin Street
Watkins Glen, NY 14891
607-535-2779

WKDT
Cadet Message Center
West Point, NY 10996
914-938-2127, 914-938-4567

WDST
118 Tinker Street
Woodstock, NY 12498
914-679-7266

Press

CMJ
830 Willis Ave.
Albertson, NY 11507
516-248-9600
Contact: Scott Byron, Jem Aswad, or
Deborah Orr

Good Times
P.O. Box 268
Greenvale, NY 11549
516-767-0312
Contact: John Blenn

Island Ear
P.O. Box 309
Island Park, NY 11558
516-889-6045
Contact: Scott Schinder

PENNSYLVANIA

Ardmore

Just outside of Philadelphia proper.

Venues

Ambler Cabaret
23 East Lancaster Ave.
Ardmore, PA 19003
215-896-6420
Contact: Greg Mountain
Three clubs, any kind of music

Plastic Fantastic Records
26 West Lancaster Ave.
Ardmore, PA 19003
215-896-7625
Contact: Dave

Record Stores

Matt's Discount Records
9 West Lancaster Ave.
Ardmore, PA 19003
215-642-0764
Contact: John Rotondi

Philadelphia

If you call any of the radio stations, you'll probably be given the name of a new, small, hip club in the university area. They change all the time — good luck.

Venues

Bacchanal
1320 South Street
Philadelphia, PA 19147
215-545-6983
Send tapes to: Pete Eshelman
910 South Farraght Terrace
Philadelphia, PA 19143
215-386-8439

Chestnut Cabaret
3801 Chestnut Street
Philadelphia, PA 19104
215-896-6420
Contact: Greg Mountain

JC Dobbs
304 South Street
Philadelphia, PA 19147
215-925-4053, 215-925-6679
Contact: Kathy James
Any kind of music

Revival
22 South Third Street
Philadelphia, PA 19106
215-627-4825

Trocadero
1003 Arch Street
Philadelphia, PA 19107
215-592-0385
Contact: Larry Goldfarb
215-574-2900

Record Stores

Chaos Records
619 South Fourth Street
Philadelphia, PA 19147
215-922-6707
Contact: John Brubaker

Discovery Discs
3417 Spruce Street
Philadelphia, PA 19104
215-387-6616
Contact: Richard Moskowitz

House of Music
Rising Sun Plaza
Philadelphia, PA 19120
215-745-3911
Contact: Joe Sulpizio

Philadelphia Record Exchange
608 South Fifth Street
Philadelphia, PA 19147
215-925-7892
Contact: J.C. Webster or Chris
Simpson

Third St. Rock and Jazz
10 North Third Street
Philadelphia, PA 19106
215-627-3366
Contact: Jerry Gordon

Tower Records
610 South Street
Philadelphia, PA 19147
215-574-9888
Contact: Greg Loop

We Three Record Shops
3900 Main Street
Philadelphia, PA 19127
215-483-9550
Contact: Howard Rosen

Radio Stations

WHYY
150 North Sixth Street
Philadelphia, PA 19106
215-351-9200

WKDU
Drexel University
3210 Chestnut Street
Philadelphia, PA 19014
215-895-2580

WMMR
19th and Walnut
Third Floor
Philadelphia, PA 19103
215-561-0933

WQHS
University of Pennsylvania
3905 Spruce Street
Philadelphia, PA 19104
215-898-9553, 215-898-3500

WRTI-Jazz 90
Temple University
Annenberg Hall
Philadelphia, PA 19122
215-787-8405

WXPN
3905 Spruce Street
Philadelphia, PA 19104
215-898-6677

Press

City Paper
206 South 13th Street
Chancellor Building Mezzanine
Philadelphia, PA 19107
215-735-8444
Contact: David Warner or Frank
Blank
Local publication with club listings

Philadelphia Inquirer
400 North Broad Street
Philadelphia, PA 19101
215-854-2000

Welcome Mat, The
1816 Ludlow Street
Philadelphia, PA 19103
215-563-7400
Contact: Derick Davis

Pittsburgh
Venues

Decade
223 Atwood Street
Pittsburgh, PA 15213
412-682-1211
Contact: Dom Disilvia
Rock 'n' roll and R & B

Graffiti Showcase Cafe
4615 Baum Blvd.
Pittsburgh, PA 15213
412-682-4210
Contact: Paul Dinardo

Record Stores

Jim's Records
4526 Liberty
Pittsburgh, PA 15224
412-621-3256
Contact: Jim Spitznagle

National Record Mart
5607 Baum Blvd.
Pittsburgh, PA 15206
412-441-4100
Contact: Frank Fisher

Oasis Records
3712 Forbes Ave.
Pittsburgh, PA 15213
412-687-9433
Contact: Mike Whited

Phantom of the Attic
214 South Craig
Pittsburgh, PA 15213
412-621-1210
Contact: Dave Martin

Radio Stations

WMXP
224 North Ave.
Pittsburgh, PA 15209
412-821-6140

WPTS
University of Pittsburgh
411 William Pitt Union
Pittsburgh, PA 15213
412-648-7990

WQED
4802 Fifth Ave.
Pittsburgh, PA 15213
412-622-1436

WRCT
Carnegie-Mellon University
5020 Forbes Ave.
Pittsburgh, PA 15213
412-621-9728

Press

In Pittsburgh
P.O. Box 4286
Pittsburgh, PA 15203
412-488-1212
Contact: Scott Mervis

Wilkes-Barre
Record Stores

Gallery of Sound
Wyoming Valley Mall
Wilkes-Barre, PA 18702
717-829-3603
Contact: Joe Nardone

Radio Stations

WCLH
Wilkes College
Wilkes-Barre, PA 18766
717-825-7663

WRKC
Kings College
133 North Franklin Street
Wilkes-Barre, PA 18711
717-826-5821

Miscellaneous Pennsylvania

Record Stores

Record Outlet
801 State Street
Lemoyne, PA 17043
717-737-6399
Contact: Wayne, Jack, or Eric

Arboria Records
151 South Allen Street
State College, PA 16801
814-237-3808
Contact: Josh

Repo Records
139 Pennyslvania Ave.
Wayne, PA 19087
215-254-0722
Contact: Dan Matherson

Radio Stations

WMUH
Muhlenberg College
P.O. Box 2806
Allentown, PA 18104
215-433-5957

WRFT
Temple University-Ambler Campus
C/O Student Services
Meetinghouse Road
Ambler, PA 19002
215-283-1278

WGEV
Geneva College
Beaver Falls, PA 15010
412-847-6678

WLVR
Lehigh University
P.O. Box 20 A
Bethlehem, PA 18015
215-758-3913

WZZO
Westgate Mall
Suite 205
Bethlehem, PA 18017
215-694-0511

WBSC
Bloomsburg University
P.O. Box 85
Kehr Union
Bloomsburg, PA 17815
717-389-4459

WBUQ
Bloomsburg University
P.O. Box 85
Kehr Union
Bloomsburg, PA 17815
717-389-4686

WVCS
California State College
428 Hickory Street
California, PA 15419
412-938-4330

WDCV
Dickinson College
P.O. Box 640
Carlisle, PA 17013
717-245-1661

WDNR
Widener University
P.O. Box 1000
Chester, PA 19013
215-499-4439

WCUC
Clarion State College
Clarion, PA 16214
814-226-2330

WESS
East Stroudsburg University
Student Center
P.O. Box 198
East Stroudsburg, PA 18301
717-424-3512

WJRH
Lafayette College
P.O. Box 4029
Easton, PA 18042
215-250-5316

WFSE
Edinboro University
Compton Hall, Room 102
Edinboro, PA 16444
814-732-2526

WERG
Gannon University
P.O. Box 236
Erie, PA 16541
814-871-7496

WZBT
Gettysburg College
P.O. Box 435
Gettysburg, PA 17325
717-337-6315

WTPA
P.O. Box 9350
Harrisburg, PA 17108
717-697-1141

WHRC
Haverford College
Haverford, PA 19041
215-649-1200

WKVR
Juniata College
P.O. Box 1005
Huntingdon, PA 16652
814-643-5031

WIUP
Indiana University of Pennsylvania
121 Stouffer Hall
Indiana, PA 15705
412-357-2490

WFNM
Franklin and Marshall College
P.O. Box 3003
Lancaster, PA 17604
717-291-4096

WVBU
Bucknell University
P.O. Box C-3028
Lewisburg, PA 17837
717-524-1326

WARC
Allegheny College
Meadville, PA 16335
814-332-3376
Contact: Carl Garrett, General
Manager; Bernadette Ksiazek,
Program Director

WIXQ
Millersville University
S.U.C. Basement
Millersville, PA 17551
717-872-3519

WVIA
Public Broadcast Center
Old Boston Road
Pittston, PA 18640
717-655-2808

WCAB
Cabrini College
Radner, PA 19087
215-971-8453

WVMW
Marywood College
2300 Adams
Scranton, PA 18509
717-348-6202

WQSU
Susquehanna University
Selinsgrove, PA 17870
717-286-8400

WSYC
Shippensburg University
Cumberland Union Building
Shippensburg, PA 17257
717-532-6006

WSRN
Swarthmore College
Swarthmore, PA 19081
215-328-8340

WEHR
Penn State University
East Hall
University Park, PA 16802
814-863-0072

WPSU
Penn State University
304 Sparks Building
University Park, PA 16802
814-865-9191

WKVU
Villanova University
Tollentine Hall
P.O. Box 105
Villanova, PA 19085
215-645-7200

WCUR
Westchester University
219 Sykes Union
Westchester, PA 19383
215-436-2477

WVYC
York College of Pennsylvania
Country Club Road
York, PA 17403-3426
717-845-7413

Press

Freedom of Expression
4992 Indian Trail Road
Northampton, PA 18067
215-262-3163
Contact: Frank Pearn Jr.

NEW ENGLAND

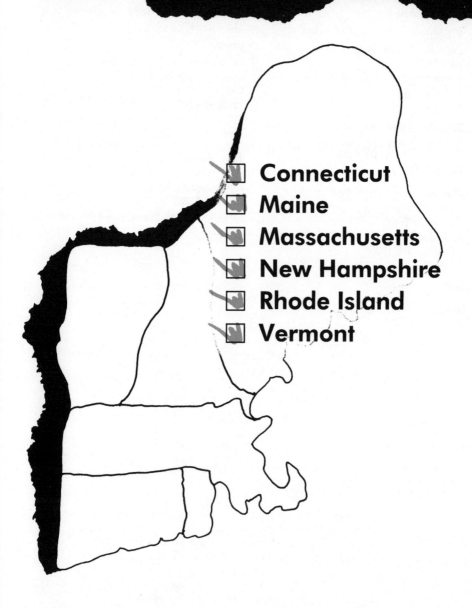

☐ Connecticut
☐ Maine
☐ Massachusetts
☐ New Hampshire
☐ Rhode Island
☐ Vermont

CONNECTICUT

Bridgeport

Record Stores

Nu Music Records
2987 Fairfield Ave.
Bridgeport, CT 06605
203-333-5919
Contact: Scott Anderson

Radio Stations

WPKN
University of Bridgeport
144 University Ave.
Bridgeport, CT 06601
203-576-4895

Hartford

Record Stores

Belltone Records
1291 Albany Ave.
Hartford, CT 06112
203-724-9136
Contact: Dwight Barrett

Record Express
983 Farmington Ave.
West Hartford, CT 06107
203-236-6683

Radio Stations

WHCN
1039 Asylum Ave.
Hartford, CT 06105
203-247-1060

WRTC-FM
Trinity College
300 Summit Street
Hartford, CT 06106
203-297-2450

WWUH
University of Hartford
200 Bloomfield Ave.
West Hartford, CT 06117
201-243-4703 or 201-243-4701

Press

Hartford Courant
285 Broad Street
Hartford, CT 06115
203-241-6200
Contact: Roger Catlin, Music Editor

New Haven

This city has a history of tension between the Ivy Leagers and the town's people. However, music is an interest that both parties can agree upon. New Haven houses a couple of hot clubs, not including the university options.

Venues

Toad's Place
300 York Street
New Haven, CT 06511
203-562-5694
Contact: Katherine Cormack

Record Stores

Cutlers Records
33 Broadway
New Haven, CT 06510
203-777-6271
Contact: Al Lotto

Rhymes Records
59 Broadway
New Haven, CT 06511
203-562-2508
Contact: Mike Taylor

Radio Stations

WNHU
C/O University of New Haven
300 Orange Ave.
West Haven, CT 06516
203-934-9296

WSCB
Southern Connecticut State
University
501 Crescent Street
New Haven, CT 06515
203-389-4457

WYBC
Yale Station
P.O. Box WYBC
165 Elm Street
New Haven, CT 06520
203-432-4116

Press

New Haven Register
40 Sargent Drive
New Haven, CT 06511
203-562-1121
Contact: Hayne Bayless

Storrs

Record Stores

Disc Records
1254 Storrs Road
Route 195
Storrs, CT 06268
203-429-0443
Contact: Martin Kelly

University Music
Route 195
University Plaza
Storrs, CT 06268
203-429-7709
Indy Buyer

Radio Stations

WHUS
University of Connecticut
P.O. Box U-8R
2110 Hillside Road
Storrs, CT 06269-3008
203-486-4007

Willimantic

Record Stores

Platter Connection
920 Main Street
Willimantic, CT 06226
203-456-7552
Contact: Joe Malinowski

Radio Stations

WECS
Eastern Connecticut State University
83 Wendham
Willimantic, CT 06226
203-456-2164

Miscellaneous Connecticut

Venues

Anthrax
25 Perry Ave.
Norwalk, CT 06850
203-849-1164
Contact: Brian
All music except mainstream and heavy metal

Record Stores

Record Breaker
336 Broad Street
Manchester, CT 06040
203-647-1495
Contact: Chack or Dave

Record Express
422 Main Street
Middletown, CT 06457
203-346-2448
Contact: Bob Duffy

Record Breaker
2188 Berlin Turnpike
Newington, CT 06111
203-666-0696
Contact: Chack or Dave

Platter Connection
2359 Main Street
Rocky Hill, CT 06067
203-257-9601
Contact: Joe Malinowski

Graf-Wadman Records
Dock Shopping Center
955 Fury Blvd.
Stratford, CT 06497
203-377-0438
Indy Buyer

Phoenix Records
84 Bank Street
Waterbury, CT 06702
203-756-1617
Contact: Professor Moronow

Integrity 'N Music
506 Silas Deane Hgwy.
Wethersfield, CT 06109
203-563-4005
Contact: Ed Krech

Radio Stations

WRKI
P.O. Box 95
Danbury, CT 06813
203-775-1212

WXCI
Western Connecticut State College
181 White Street
Danbury, CT 06810
203-744-5402

WSHU
Sacred Heart University
5151 Park Ave.
Fairfield, CT 06432
203-371-7989

WVOF
P.O. Box R
Fairfield University
North Benson Road
Fairfield, CT 06430
203-254-4111

WPLR
1191 Dixwell Ave.
Hamden, CT 06514
203-287-9070

WQAQ
Quinnipiac College
555 New Road
Hamden, CT 06518
203-281-0011

WESU-FM
Wesleyan College
2300 Wesleyan Station
Middletown, CT 06457
203-347-0050

WFCS
Central Connecticut State College
1615 Stanley Street
New Britain, CT 06050
203-223-6767

WCNI
Connecticut College
P.O. Box 1333
New London, CT 06320
203-444-1849

MAINE

Miscellaneous Maine

Venues

Tree Cafe
45 Danforth
Portland, ME 04101
207-774-1441
Contact: Tom Dansmore or Herb
Gideon
All kinds of music

Geno's
Downtown Station
Portland, ME 04112
207-772-9521
Contact: Geno or Richard
Mailing Address: P.O. Box 106
Portland, ME 04112
No heavy metal

Radio Stations

WBOR
Bowdoin College
Moulton Union
Brunswick, ME 04011
207-725-5008

WUMF
University of Maine
86 Main Street
Farmington, ME 04938
207-778-4522

WMPG
37 College Ave.
Gorham, ME 04038
207-780-5415

WRBC
Bates College
31 Frye Street
Lewiston, ME 04240
207-784-9722, 207-784-9340

WMEB
University of Maine
East Annex
Orono, ME 04469
207-581-2333

WUPI
181 Main Street
Presque Isle, ME 04769
207-764-0311, X309

WTOS
P.O. Box 159
Skowhegan, ME 04976
207-474-5171

WMHB
Colby College
Roberts Union
Waterville, ME 04901
207-872-8037

WSJB
St. Joseph's College
Windham, ME 04062-1198
207-892-2266

MASSACHUSETTS

Allston

Boston has a happening music scene, offering a wide variety of clubs (sizes, hiring practics, clientele, and age groups). The Amherst area has several colleges that occasionally hire bands. Furthermore, don't overlook the large number of college radio stations in Massachusetts. The radio play possibilities are endless.

Venues

Bunratty's
186 Harvard Ave.
Allston, MA 02134
617-254-9804, 617-254-9820
Contact: David, Entertainment
Department
Any kind of music

Press

Beat, The
8A Glenville Ave.
Allston, MA 02134
617-782-7625, 617-782-ROCK
Contact: Michael Hill, Editor
Same people run Bunratty's

Amherst

Record Stores

For The Record
159 North Pleasant Street
Amherst, MA 01002
413-256-6134
Contact: Wylie Smith

WMUA
University of Massachusetts
102 Campus Center
Amherst, MA 01003
413-545-2876

Radio Stations

WAMH
Amherst College
P.O. Box 1815
Amherst, MA 01002
413-542-2224, 413-542-2195

Boston

Six universities are located in this city, and the music scene thrives on it. Sometimes it's hard for a nonlocal band without a big name to get a gig and be received, but it's worth the try.

Venues

Axis
13 Lansdowne Street
Boston, MA 02215
617-262-2437
Contact: Jeff Marshall
Progressive rock

Channel, The
25 Neco Street
Boston, MA 02210
617-451-1050
Contact: Warren or Dave. Also booked through the Entertainment Network:
137 South Street, Second Floor
Boston, MA 02111
617-426-3888
Contact: Michael Carr

Paradise
967 Commonwealth
Boston, MA 02115
617-254-2053
Any kind of music

Rat, The
528 Commonwealth Ave.
Boston, MA 02115
617-437-0684
Contact: Julie, or Lois McGee
Source talent

Record Stores

In Your Ear Records
1030 Commonwealth Ave.
Boston, MA 02215
617-739-1236
Contact: Reid Lappin

Newberry Comics
332 Newbury Street
Boston, MA 02215
617-236-4930
Contact: Natalie Werlin

Planet Records
536 Commonwealth Ave.
Boston, MA 02215
617-353-0693
Contact: John Damroth

Tower Records
360 Newbury Street
Boston, MA 02215
617-247-5900
Contact: Chris Toppin

Radio Stations

WBCN
1265 Boylston Street
Boston, MA 02215
617-266-1111

WECB
Emerson College
126 Beacon Street
Boston, MA 02128
617-578-8850

WERS
Emerson College
126 Beacon Street
Boston, MA 02116
617-578-8892

WRBB
Northeastern University
360 Huntington Ave.
Boston, MA 02115
617-367-3136, 617-437-2000

WSFR
Suffolk University
41 Temple Street
Boston, MA 02114
617-573-8000

WTBU
Boston University
640 Commonwealth Ave.
Boston, MA 02215
617-353-6400

WUMB
University of Massachusetts-Boston
Harbor Campus
Boston, MA 02125-3393
617-929-7919

Press

Boston Herald
1 Herald Square
Boston, MA 02106
617-426-3000
Contact: Larry Katz

Boston Phoenix
126 Brookline
Boston, MA 02215
617-536-5390
Contact: Myla Miles, Editor

Boston Rock
New Town Branch
P.O. Box 371
Boston, MA 02258
617-734-7043, 617-244-6803
All music magazine

Cambridge

Venues

Nightstage
823 Main Street
Cambridge, MA 02139
617-497-8200

TT The Bears
10 Brookline Ave.
Cambridge, MA 02139
617-492-0082
Contact: Bonnie Connelly or Jodi Goodman

Record Stores

Harvard Coop
1400 Massachusetts Ave.
Cambridge, MA 02238
617-492-1000
Contact: Linda Stellinger

Newbury Comics
36 JFK Street
Cambridge, MA 02138
617-491-0337
Contact: Natalie Werlin

Skippy White's
555 Massachusetts Ave.
Cambridge, MA 02139
617-491-3345
Contact: Skippy White

Radio Stations

WHRB
45 Quincy Street
Cambridge, MA 02138
617-495-4818

WMBR
Massachusetts Institute of Technology
3 Ames Street
Cambridge, MA 02142
617-253-4000

Framingham

Record Stores

Newbury Comics
341 Cochituate Road
Route 30
Framingham, MA 01701
508-620-0735
Contact: Natalie Werlin
36 JFK Street
Harvard Square
Cambridge, MA 02138

Radio Stations

WDJM
Framingham State College
100 State Street
Framingham, MA 01701
508-626-4623

Newburyport

Venues

Grog, The
13 Middle Street
Newburyport, MA 01950
508-465-8008
Contact: Doug Johnson
Send tapes — all styles

Record Stores

Erunzo Records
25 Inn Street, Basement
Newburyport, MA 01950
508-462-5209

Northampton

Record Stores

Mainstreet Records
213 Main Street
Northampton, MA 01060
413-586-5726
Contact: Ken Reed or Bill McDonald

Radio Stations

WOZQ
Smith College
Northampton, MA 01063
413-584-7011

Press

Daily Hampshire Gazette
115 Conz Street
Northampton, MA 01060
413-584-5000
Contact: Mariette Pritchard

Worcester

Venues

Club, The
90 Commercial Street
Worcester, MA 01608
508-754-2248
Contact: Danimal Entertainment
174 Grand Street
Worcester, MA 01603
Rock 'n' roll, jazz, and blues

McGillicuddy's
23 Foster Street
Worcester, MA 01610
508-756-6942
Contact: Helen Hughes
Rock 'n' roll

Ralph's Chadwick Square Diner
1 Diner Alley
Worchester, MA 01606
508-753-9543
Contact: Carol

Tamany Hall
43 Pleasant Street
Worcester, MA 01608
508-791-6550
Contact: John Welsh

Radio Stations

WCHC
Holy Cross College
1 College Street
Worcester, MA 01610
508-793-2471

WCUW
910 Main Street
Worcester, MA 01610
508-753-1012

WICN
6 Chatham Street
Worcester, MA 01609
508-752-7517

WSCW
Worcester State College
486 Chandler Street
Worcester, MA 01602
508-793-8000

Miscellaneous Massachusetts

Venues

Grovers
392 Cabot Street
Beverly, MA 01915
508-922-8867

Edible Rex
251 Olde Concord
Billerica, MA 01821
508-667-6393
Contact: Michael Reck

Tam O'Shanter, The
1648 Beacon Street
Brookline, MA 02146
617-277-0982

Contact: Michael
C/O P.O. Box 1110
Brookline, MA 02146
R & B and some rock 'n' roll

Green Street Station, The
131 Green Street
Jamaica Plain, MA 02130
617-522-0792
Contact: Joyce Linehan
617-436-7209
Rock 'n' roll and blues

Club III
608 Somerville Ave.
Somerville, MA 02144
617-623-6957
Contact: Valerie
Rock 'n' roll

Johnny D's
17 Holland Street
Somerville, MA 02144
617-776-2004
Contact: Karla, or Jon Peters
All kinds of rock 'n' roll, blues, and reggae

Record Stores

Wex Rex Records
P.O. Box 702
Hudson, MA 01749
508-568-0856
Contact: Gary Sohmers

Cambridge One Stop
205 Fortune Blvd.
Milford, MA 01757
508-478-2031
Indy Buyer

Strawberries Records
435 Boston Post Road
Sudbury, MA 01776
508-443-8933

Cambridge One Stop
205 Fortune Blvd.
Milford, MA 01757
508-478-2031

Radio Stations

WBIM
Bridgewater State College
Student Union Building
Bridgewater, MA 02324
508-697-1303

WZBC
Boston College
P.O. Box K151
McElroy Commons
Chestnut Hill, 02167
617-552-4686

WGAJ
Deerfield Academy
P.O.Box 248
Deerfield, MA 01342
413-773-8412

WNRC
c/o Nichols College
Dudley, MA 01570
508-943-8320

WCIB
P.O. Box C
Falmouth, MA 02541
508-548-3102

WXPL
Fitchburg State College, Hammond Building
160 Pearl Street
Fitchburg, MA 01420
617-345-0276

WRSI
Green Valley Broadcasting
P.O. Box 910
Greenfield, MA 01302
413-774-2321

WCCH
Holyoke Community College
303 Homestead Ave.
Holyoke, MA 01040
413-536-5201

WJUL
University of Lowell
1 University Ave.
Lowell, MA 01854
508-459-0579

WMFO
Tufts University
490 Boston Ave.
Medford, MA 02153
617-625-0800

WMLN
Curry College
1071 Blue Hill Ave.
Milton, MA 02186
617-333-0311

WJJW
North Adams State College
Campus Center
North Adams, MA 01247
413-663-9136

WUSM
South Eastern Massachusetts
University
Old Westport Road
North Dartmouth, MA 02747
508-999-8174

WSHL
Stonehill College
320 Washington Ave.
North Easton, MA 02357
508-238-2612

WBEC
P.O. Box 958
Pittsfield, MA 01201
413-499-3333

WTBR
Valentine Road
Pittsfield, MA 01201
413-499-1483

WMWM
Salem State College
352 Lafayette Street
Salem, MA 01970
508-745-9401

WMHC
P.O. Box 1764
Mount Holyoke College
South Hadley, MA 01075
413-538-2044

WAIC
American International College
1000 State Street
Springfield, MA 01109
413-736-7662

WNEK
Western New England College
1215 Wilbraham Road
Springfield, MA 01119
413-782-1582

WSCB
Springfield College
263 Alden Street
Springfield, MA 01109
413-732-1000

WTCC
Springfield Tech
1 Armory Square
Springfield, MA 01105
413-781-6629

WBRS
Brandeis University
415 South Street
Waltham, MA 02254
617-736-4785

WBTY
Bentley College
Waltham, MA 02254
617-891-3473

WZLY
Wellesley College
106 Central Street
Wellesley, MA 02181-9980
617-235-9150

WKKL
Cape Cod Community College
Route 132
West Barnstable, MA 02668
508-362-4941

WSKB
Westfield State College
577 Western Ave.
Westfield, MA 01086
413-568-3311

WCFM
William College
Baxter Hall
Williamstown, MA 01267
413-597-2373

Press

Boston Globe
135 William T. Morrissey Blvd.
Dorchester, MA 02067
617-929-2810
Contact: Steve Morse, Music Editor

Valley Advocate
87 School Street
Hatfield, MA 01038
413-247-9301
Contact: David Sokol

Tab, The
1238 Chestnut Street
Newton, MA 02164
617-964-2400
Contact: Ed Symkus, Music Editor

Forced Exposure
719 Washington Street #172
Newtonville, MA 02160
617-924-3923
Contact: Jimmy Johnson
Quarterly fanzine

Suburban Voice
56 Lewis Road
Swampscott, MA 01907
617-596-1570
Contact: Al Quin
Bi-monthly fanzine

N E W   H A M P S H I R E

Durham

Venues

University of New Hampshire
MUSU Memorial Union Building
Durham, NH 03824
603-862-1485
Contact: Eric Stites
All kinds of music

Radio Stations

WUNH
University of New Hampshire
Memorial Union Building
Durham, NH 03824
603-862-2541

Portsmouth

Record Stores

Rock Bottom Records
86 Pleasant Street
Portsmouth, NH 03801
603-436-5618
Contact: Kevin Guyer

Radio Stations

WHEB
P.O. Box 120
Portsmouth, NH 03801
603-436-7300

Miscellaneous New Hampshire

Venues

Decadence
P.O. Box 734
Rollingsford, NH 03869
603-742-0042
Contact: Randy Kilty
National acts and top 40

White Horse
Route 101A
Nashwa Street
Milford, NH 03055
603-673-9831
Contact: Larry Miller

Stone Church
New Market, NH 03857
603-659-6321
Contact: Rick Hurd
Rock 'n' roll, acoustic, blues, and dance
music. No top 40 and no heavy metal.
Mailing Address: P.O. Box 202
New Market, NH 03857

Meadowbrook Inn, The
Interstate Hgwy. Circle
Portsmouth, NH 03801
603-436-2700
Contact: Doris Burt

Record Stores

Inner Light Records
10 Lake Ave.
Manchester, NH 03101
603-669-5181
Contact: Cathy Maesk

Big City Records
300 Main Street
Nashua, NH 03060
603-880-1842
Contact: Phil Desmarais

Rocket Records
293 Daniel Webster Hgwy.
Nashua, NH 03060
603-888-8441
Contact: Lee Stein

Rainbow Records
386 South Broadway
Salem, NH 03079
603-898-2143
Contact: Michael Behm

Radio Stations

WNEC
New England College
H. Wayland Danforth Library
Henniker, NH 03242
603-428-2278

WPCR
Plymouth Street College
Plymouth, NH 03264
603-536-1760

WKXL
P.O. Box 875
Concord, NH 03302-0875
603-225-5521

WKNH
Keene State College
229 Main Street
Eliot Hall
Keene, NH 03431
603-352-1909, X387

WMDK
P.O. Box 389
Route 1, Ames Court
Peterborough, NH 03458
603-924-7165

WFPR
Franklin Pierce College
College Road
Rindge, NH 03461
603-899-5111, X225

WDCR/WFRD
Dartmouth College
P.O. Box 957
Hanover, NH 03755
603-646-3313

RHODE ISLAND

Newport

Venues

Blue Pelican
Newport, RI 02840
401-847-5675
Mailing Address:
P.O. Box 3351, Broadway Station
Newport, RI 02840
Dance music, blues, and progressive rock

Record Stores

Doo Wop Records
38 Broadway
Newport, RI 02840
401-849-6496
Contact: Jim Barr

Providence

Venues

Lupo's Heartbreak Hotel
377 Westminster Mall
Providence, RI 02903
401-351-7927
Contact: Doug, Rich, or Jack

Rocket
73 Richmond Street
Providence, RI 02903
401-273-9619
Contact: James
All kinds of music

As 220
71 Richmond Street
Providence, RI 02903
401-831-9327
Contact: Umberto Crenca
All original kinds of music

Living Room
273 Promenade Street
Providence, RI 02908
401-521-2520
Contact: Randy Hien
All kinds of music

Record Stores

In Your Ear Records
171 Angel Street, Second Floor
Providence, RI 02906
401-861-1515
Contact: Chris Zingg

Tom's Tracks/Records
287 Phayer Street
Providence, RI 02906
401-274-0820
Contact: Tom Farnsworth

Fast Forward Records
200 Washington Street
Providence, RI 02903
401-272-8866
Contact: Ron Marinick

Radio Stations

WBRU
Brown University
88 Benevolent Street
Providence, RI 02906
401-272-9550

WXIN
Rhode Island College
Student Union Building
Providence, RI 02908
401-456-8288

WDOM
Providence College
River Ave.
Providence, RI 02918
401-865-2460

Press

Phoenix's New Paper
131 Washington Street
Providence, RI 02903
401-273-6397
Contact: Lou Papineau, Music Editor

Miscellaneous Rhode Island

Record Stores

Looney Tunes Records
22 Dale Carlia Street
Heritage Mall
Wakefield, RI 02879
401-789-8188
Contact: Jeff Gardner

Midland Records
281 Rhode Island Mall
Warwick, RI 02886
401-828-5850
Indy Buyer

WRIU
University of Rhode Island
Memorial Union
Kingston, RI 02881
401-792-4349, 401-789-4949

WJMF
Bryant College
450 Douglas Pike
Smithfield, RI 02917-1284
401-232-6044

Radio Stations

WQRI
Roger Williams College
Old Ferry Road
Bristol, RI 02809
401-253-0350

VERMONT

Burlington

A good stop on the way to Montreal, Canada, from the Eastern seaboard cities.

Venues

Border Club
Burlington, VT
802-864-0107
Contact: Allpoints Booking
182 Main Street #16
Burlington, VT 05401

Front, The
201 Main Street
Burlington, VT 05401
802-658-5631

Record Stores

Pure Pop Records
115 South Winooski Ave.
Burlington, VT 05401
802-658-2652
Contact: Jay Strausser

Radio Stations

WRUV
Billings Student Center
University of Vermont
489 Main Street
Burlington, VT 05405
802-656-4399

Press

Burlington Free Press
191 College Street
Burlington, VT 05401
802-863-3441
Contact: Steve Mease, Music Editor

Vanguard Press
87 College Street
Burlington, VT 05402
802-864-0506
Contact: Rick Kisonak

Montpelier

Record Stores

Buch Spieler Records
27 Langdon Street
Montpelier, VT 05602
802-229-0449
Contact: Fred Wilber

Radio Stations

WNCS
P.O. Box 551
Montpelier, VT 05602
802-223-2396

Miscellaneous Vermont

Venues

Flat Street
17 Flat Street
Brattleboro, VT 05301
802-254-8257
Contact: Jim Harris

Valley Club, The
Rutland, VT 05701
802-775-3474
Contact: Bob Alexander
P.O. Box 416
Rutland, VT 05701
No heavy metal or country

Record Stores

Exile on Main Street/Records
201 North Main Street
Barre, VT 05641
802-479-3107
Contact: Steve Sawyer or Mike
Thurston

Radio Stations

WIUV
Castleton Street College
Campus Center
Castleton, VT 05753
802-468-5611

WJSC
Johnson State College
Johnson, VT 05656
802-635-2314

WWLR
Lyndon State College
P.O. Box F
Lyndonville, VT 05851
802-626-9371

WEQX
P.O. Box 1027
Manchester, VT 05254
802-362-4800

WRMC
Middlebury College
Drawer 29
Middlebury, VT 05753
802-388-6323

WGDR
Goddard College Community Radio
Plainfield, VT 05667
802-454-7762

WRFB
P.O. Box 26
Stowe, VT 05672
802-253-4877

WIZN
The Steven's House
Vergennes, VT 05491
802-877-6800

WVPR/WVPS
107.9 Ethan Allen Ave.
Winooski, VT 05404
802-655-9451

WWPV
St. Michael College
Sloane Arts Center
Winooski, VT 05404
802-655-2000, X2338

ALASKA&
HAWAII

■ Alaska
■ Hawaii

A L A S K A

Juneau

Record Stores

Budget Tapes and Records
Nugget Mall
Juneau, AK 99801
907-789-3472
Contact: Kelly Miller

Radio Stations

KTOO
224 Fourth Street
Juneau, AK 99801
907-586-1670

Miscellaneous Alaska

Record Stores

Alaska Audio Video
P.O. Box 258
Douglas, AK 99824
907-789-8355
Contact: Bob Deckrash

KUAC
University of Alaska
Fairbanks, Alaska 99775
907-474-7491

Radio Stations

KWHL
9200 Lake Otis Pkwy.
Anchorage, AK 99507
907-344-9622

H A W A I I

Honolulu

Venues

Hard Rock Cafe
1837 Kapiolani Blvd.
Honolulu, HI 96826
808-955-7383
Occasional live entertainment

Wave-Waikiki
1877 Kalakaua Ave.
Honolulu, HI 96815
808-941-0424
Live progressive rock and new wave

Record Stores

Tower Records
611 Keeamouka Street
Honolulu, HI 96814
808-941-7774
Indy Buyer

Radio Stations

KHPR
1335 Lower Campus Drive
Honolulu, HI 96822
808-955-8821

KPOI
741 Bishop Street
Honolulu, HI 96815
808-524-7100

KTUH
University of Hawaii
2445 Campus Road #202
Honolulu, HI 96822
808-948-7431

Miscellaneous Hawaii

Radio Stations

KOAS
P.O. Box 845
Kealakekua, HI 96750
808-323-2200

CANADA

☑ British Columbia
☑ Ontario
☑ Quebec
☑ Nova Scotia

B R I T I S H C O L U M B I A

Vancouver

Canada is an option that many people in the music business overlook. Actually, it offers a great opportunity for bands to break into a market that differs from the United States. As a rule, Canadians, unlike a great number of Americans, are willing to listen to music that has not been approved by millions. In fact, Canada seems to be overflowing with music enthusiasts. The list we have included covers cities of the eastern provinces. Like most countries, Canada requires aliens to acquire work permits and make a deposit on their trade equipment. This information can be obtained from any Canadian immigration office. If several gigs are landed, the cost is minimal. We suggest making arrangements to borrow as much equipment as possible in Canada. This can bring the deposit down (it sometimes takes the Canadian government up to three months to return your deposit). Canadian immigration is nothing to fear (if you're not trying to smuggle any goodies across the border). Promoters put on a lot of independent shows and are very valuable resources. The Canadian people are very hospitable and the seafood of the coastal provinces is cheap and delicious. So good luck, eh.

Venues

88 Street
Music Hall
750 Pacific Blvd.
Vancouver, British Columbia V6B 5E7
604-683-8687
Contact: Elaine Chick
All kinds of music, from Western to Brian Adams

Arts Club Lounge
1181 Seymour Street
Vancouver, British Columbia V6B 3N1
604-683-0151
Contact: David Harrison
All kinds of music

Club Soda
1055 Homer
Vancouver, British Columbia V6B 2X5
604-681-8202
Contact: Jackie Ford
Rock 'n' roll but different venues each night

Commodore
870 Granville Street
Vancouver, British Columbia V6Z 1K3
604-681-7838
Contact: Drew Burns
All varieties of music

Graceland
1250 Richards
Vancouver, British Columbia V6B 3G4
604-688-2648
Contact: Neil McPherson

Railway Club
579 Dunsmuir Street
Vancouver, British Columbia V6B 1Y4
604-681-1828

Roxy
332 Granville Street
Vancouver, British Columbia V6Z 1L2
604-684-7699
Contact: Blain Culling
Classic rock 'n' roll

Smilin' Buddha
109 East Hastings
Vancouver, British Columbia
604-889-3138

Town Pump
66 Water Street
Vancouver, British Columbia V6B 1A4
604-683-6695
Contact: Bob Burrows
All kinds of music, but no cover bands

Waterfront
686 Powell
Vancouver, British Columbia
604-253-6753

Record Stores

Main St. Records
947 Granville Street
Vancouver, British Columbia V6Z 1L3
604-685-1055
Contact: Gills Roy

Neptoon Records
5750 Fraser Street
Vancouver, British Columbia B5W 2Z5
604-324-1229
Contact: Rob Frith

Odyssey Imports
534 Seymour
Vancouver, British Columbia B6B 3J5
604-669-6644
Indy Buyer

Track Records
552 Seymour Street
Vancouver, British Columbia V6B 3J5
604-682-7976
Contact: Phil Sanesbury or Alan Hampton

Zulu Records
1869 West Fourth Ave.
Vancouver, British Columbia V6J 1M4
604-738-3232
Contact: Grant McDonagh

Radio Stations

CITR-RA
Student Union Building, Room 233
6138 South Blvd.
Vancouver, British Columbia V6T 2A5
604-228-3017

CJIV
Simon Fraser University
TC 216
Vancouver, British Columbia V5A 1S6
604-291-4423

Vancouver Cooperative Radio
337 Carrall
Vancouver, British Columbia V6B 2J4
604-684-8494

Press

Georgia Straight
1235 West Pender, Second Floor
Vancouver, British Columbia V6E 2V6
604-681-2000
Contact: Charles Campbell

Nite Moves
201-109 Carroll
Vancouver, British Columbia V6B 2H9
604-688-4610
Contact: Bob Colebrook

Province, The
2250 Granville Street
Vancouver, British Columbia V6H 3G2
604-736-2261
Contact: Tom Harris

Vancouver Sun, The
2250 Granville Street
Vancouver, British Columbia V6H
3G2
604-732-2445
Contact: John Mackie

Victoria

Record Stores

A and B Sound
641 Yates Street
Victoria, British Columbia V8W 1L2
604-385-1461
Contact: Brian Orr

Catapult Records
101-561 Johnson Street
Victoria, British Columbia V8W 1M2
604-386-2115
Contact: Kerry McPherson

Groovy Times Distribution
3217 Quadra Street
Victoria, British Columbia V8X 1G4
604-383-1669

Lyle's Place
768 Yates Street
Victoria, British Columbia V8W 1L4
604-382-8422
Contact: Jamie Fulton

Mezzrow's Records
3625 Douglas Street
Victoria, British Columbia V8Z 3L6
604-381-2633
Contact: Derwin Towell

Sweet Thunder Records
575 Johnson Street
Victoria, British Columbia V8W 1M2
604-381-4042
Contact: Shaukat Husain

Radio Stations

CFUV
University of Victoria
P.O. Box 1700
Victoria, British Columbia V8W 2Y2
604-721-8702

O N T A R I O

Guelph

Venues

C.S.A. University Center
University of Guelph, Second Level
Guelph, Ontario N1G 2W1
519-824-4120
Contact: John

Radio Stations

CFRU
University of Guelph
University Centre, Level 2
Guelph, Ontario N1G 2W1
519-824-4120, X6919

Ottawa

Venues

Barrymore's
323 Bank Street
Ottawa, Ontario K2P 1X9
613-238-5842
Contact: Gordon Kent
Any kind of music

CKCU-FM
Carleton University
Unicentre, Room 517
Ottawa, Ontario K1S 5B6
613-564-2898

Radio Stations

CFUO
University of Ottawa
85 University Street, Suite 227
Ottawa, Ontario K1N 6N5
613-564-2903

Toronto

"We are not the most open-minded audience; in fact, we are pretty critical of new music, whether it's an American group or Canadian. But when it's good, we really like it." —I.O. Perry, Toronto Resident

Venues

Bamboo Club, The
312 Queen Street West
Toronto, Ontario M5V 2A2
416-593-5771
Contact: Richard O'Brien
African, reggae, and jazz

Cabana Club, The
460 King Street West
Toronto, Ontario M5V 1L7
416-368-2864
Contact: Jim Scopies
All kinds of music — rock 'n' roll, country and jazz

Cameron Public House
408 Queens Street West
Toronto, Ontario M5V 2A7
416-364-0811
Contact: Cindy Mathews
Original music

Horseshoe Tavern
370 Queen Street West
Toronto, Ontario M5V 2A2
416-598-4753

RPM
132 Queens Street East
Toronto, Ontario M5A 3Y5
416-869-1462
Contact: Murry

Record Stores

Cheapies Records
323 Yonge Street
Toronto, Ontario M5B 1R7
416-596-6967
Contact: Jim Summers

Cheapies Records
599A Yonge Street
Toronto, Ontario M4Y 1Z5
416-924-4606
Contact: David George

Record Peddler
12 Brant Street
Toronto, Ontario M5V 2M1
416-364-5507
Contact: Angus

Record Peddler
45 Carlton Street
Toronto, Ontario M5B 1L2
416-977-7674
Contact: Brian Taylor

Radio Stations

CIUT
University of Toronto
91 St. George Street
Toronto, Ontario M5F 2E8
416-595-0909

CKLN
380 Victoria Street
Toronto, Ontario M5B 1W7
416-595-1477

Q U E B E C

Montreal

Venues

Cafe Campus
870 Delagauehegiere East
Montreal, Quebec H2L 2N2
514-842-7550
Contact: Mark Frazier

Club Soda
5240 Park Ave.
Montreal, Quebec H2V 4G7
514-270-7848
*Booked through Fogel Sabourin
Productions
Any kind of music*

Station 10
2071 St. Katherine Street West
Montreal, Quebec H3H 1M6
514-934-0484
Contact: Casey

Radio Stations

CKUT
3480 McTavish, Suite B-15
Montreal, Quebec 83A 1X9
514-398-6787

Press

Gazette
250 St. Antoine Street West
Montreal, Quebec H2Y 3R7
514-282-2222
Contact: Mark Lepage

NOVA SCOTIA

Halifax

Venues

Club Flamingo
Maratime Center
1505 Barrington
Halifax, Nova Scotia B3J 3K5
902-425-2801
Contact: Keith Tufts
One of the best places to play in North America

Radio Stations

CKDU-FM
Dalhousie Student Union
6136 University Ave.
Halifax, Nova Scotia B3H 4J2
902-424-6479

Miscellaneous Canada

Record Stores

Star Records
148 Sincoe Street South
Oshawa, Ontario L1H 4G7
416-723-0040
Contact: Mike Shulga

Trend Distributors
47 Racine Road 1 #6
Rexdale, Ontario M9W 6B2
416-749-6601
Contact: Jerry Hawkman

Radio Stations

CFNY
83 Kennedy Road South
Brampton, Ontario L6W 3P3
416-453-7452

CJSW
University of Calgary
Room 118, Macewan Hall
Calgary, Alberta T2N 1N4
403-220-3903

CJSR
University of Alberta
Room 224, Sub
Edmonton, Alberta T6G 2J7
403-432-5244

CHIM
3805 Lakeshore Road
Kelowna, British Columbia V1Y 7V2
604-762-3331

CKUL
University of Lethbridge
4401 University Drive
Lethbridge, Alberta T1K 3M4
403-329-2335

CHRW
University of Western Ontario
University Community Center,
Room 222
London, Ontario N6A 3K7
519-679-2239

CHRY
258A Vanaer College
York University
4700 Keele Street
North York, Ontario M3J 1P3
416-736-5293

CFFF
Trent University
Peterborough, Ontario K9J 7B8
705-748-1777

CKRL
47 Ste. Ursule
Quebec City, Quebec G1R 4E4
418-692-2575

CHMR-FM
Memorial University
P.O. Box A-119
St. John's, Newfoundland A1C 5S7
709-737-4777

CJAM
University of Windsor
401 Sunset Ave.
Windsor, Ontario N9B 3P4
519-258-6397

CKIC
Acadia University
P.O. Box 1269
Wolfville, Nova Scotia B0P 1X0
902-542-2287, X(1)37

CITY INDEX

NOTES

iLAVE
Jordan Seaman

NOTES

NOTES

NOTES

NOTES

NOTES

Other Books to Help You Make Money and the Most of Your Music Talent

The Craft & Business of Songwriting, by John Braheny — A powerful, information-packed (and the most up-to-date) book about the songwriting industry which thoroughly covers all the creative and business aspects that you need to know to maximize your chances of success. 322 pages/$19.95

The Craft of Lyric Writing, by Sheila Davis — Davis, a successful lyricist, composer, and teacher, presents the theory, principles, and techniques that result in lyrics with timeless appeal. 350 pages/$18.95

Successful Lyric Writing: A Step-by-Step Course & Workbook, by Sheila Davis — A practical, self-contained lyric writing course, complete with exercises and lyric writing assignments designed to stimulate your creativity and build writing skills. 304 pages/$16.95, paperback

Getting Noticed: A Musician's Guide to Publicity & Self-Promotion, by James Gibson — Gibson helps performing musicians create effective yet inexpensive publicity materials, then use them to *get noticed* and *make money* with their music. 224 pages/$12.95, paperback

Making Money Making Music (No Matter Where You Live), by James Dearing — Dearing shows you how to build a successful music career in any community — playing clubs, performing radio and TV jingles, operating a record studio, teaching, and selling lyrics through the mail. 305 pages/$12.95, paperback

The Performing Artist's Handbook, by Janice Papolos — Practical know-how classical musicians need to progress in their professional music careers. 219 pages/$10.95, paperback

The Songwriter's Guide to Making Great Demos, by Harvey Rachlin — From how to judge if a song is ready to be pitched to exactly how to produce a multi-track recording, covers every step of the process of making great demos. 192 pages/$12.95, paperback

Making It in the New Music Business, by James Riordan — The coauthor of *The Platinum Rainbow* shows how to achieve success as a recording artist by building your own path to success. 377 pages/$18.95

The Songwriter's Guide to Collaboration, by Walter Carter — A complete guide to all aspects of co-writing songs, from working relationships to legal and financial arrangements. 178 pages/$12.95, paperback

How to Pitch & Promote Your Songs, by Fred Koller—For song-writers who want to make a full-time living with their music, a step-by-step self-employment guide. 144 pages/$12.95, paperback

Writing Music for Hit Songs, by Jai Josefs—A definitive guide to composing hit songs, including more than 150 examples from today's rock, R&B, pop, and country artists. 224 pages/$16.95

A complete catalog of all Writer's Digest Books is available FREE by writing to the address shown below. To order books directly from the publisher, include $2.50 postage and handling for one book, 50¢ for each additional book. Allow 30 days for delivery.

Writer's Digest Books
1507 Dana Avenue
Cincinnati, Ohio 45207

Credit card orders call TOLL-FREE
1-800-543-4644 (Outside Ohio)
1-800-551-0884 (Ohio only)

Prices subject to change without notice